I0410065

The World of

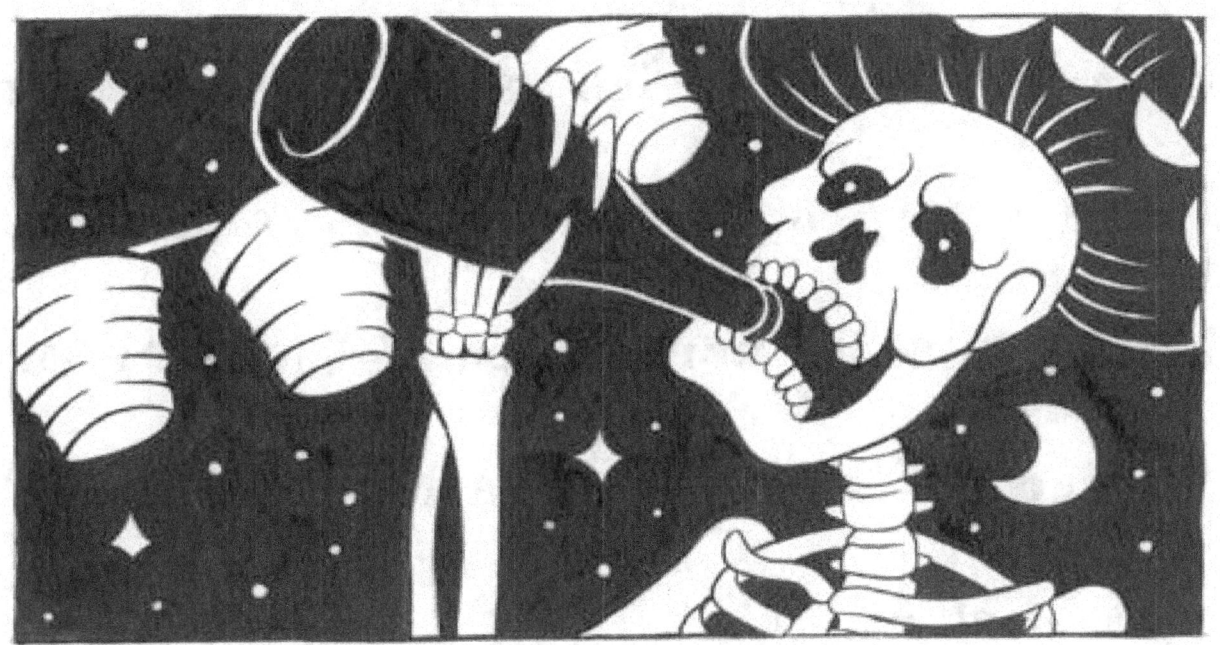

Michael D'Orazio

Volume 2

Copyright 2012 by Michael D'Orazio.

All rights reserved. No part of this book may

Be used or reproduced in any manner whatsoever

Without written permission of the publisher.

Published by Michael D'Orazio's Gallery.

You can find me at:

MichaelDOraziosGallery.com

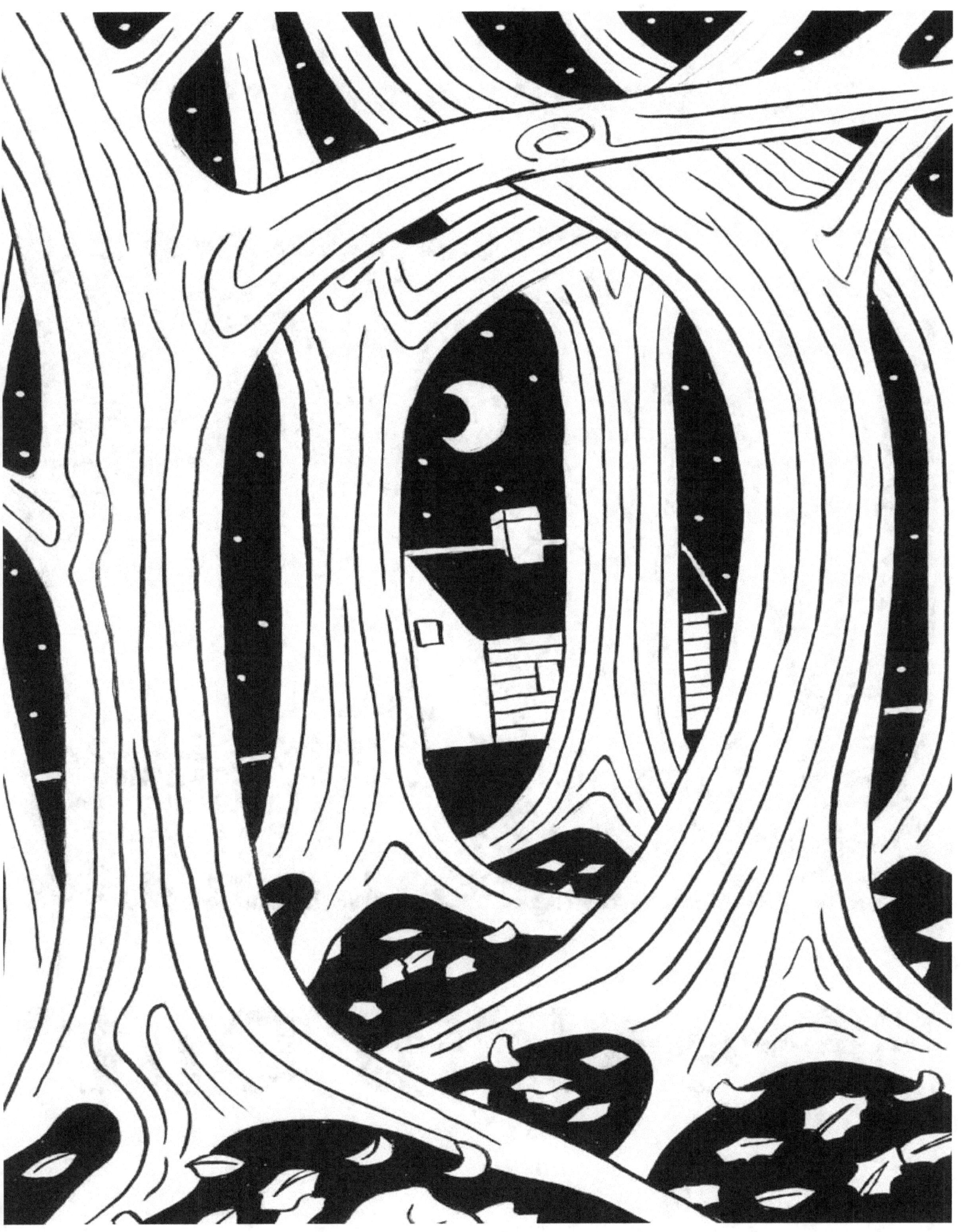

"Loonier than Looney"

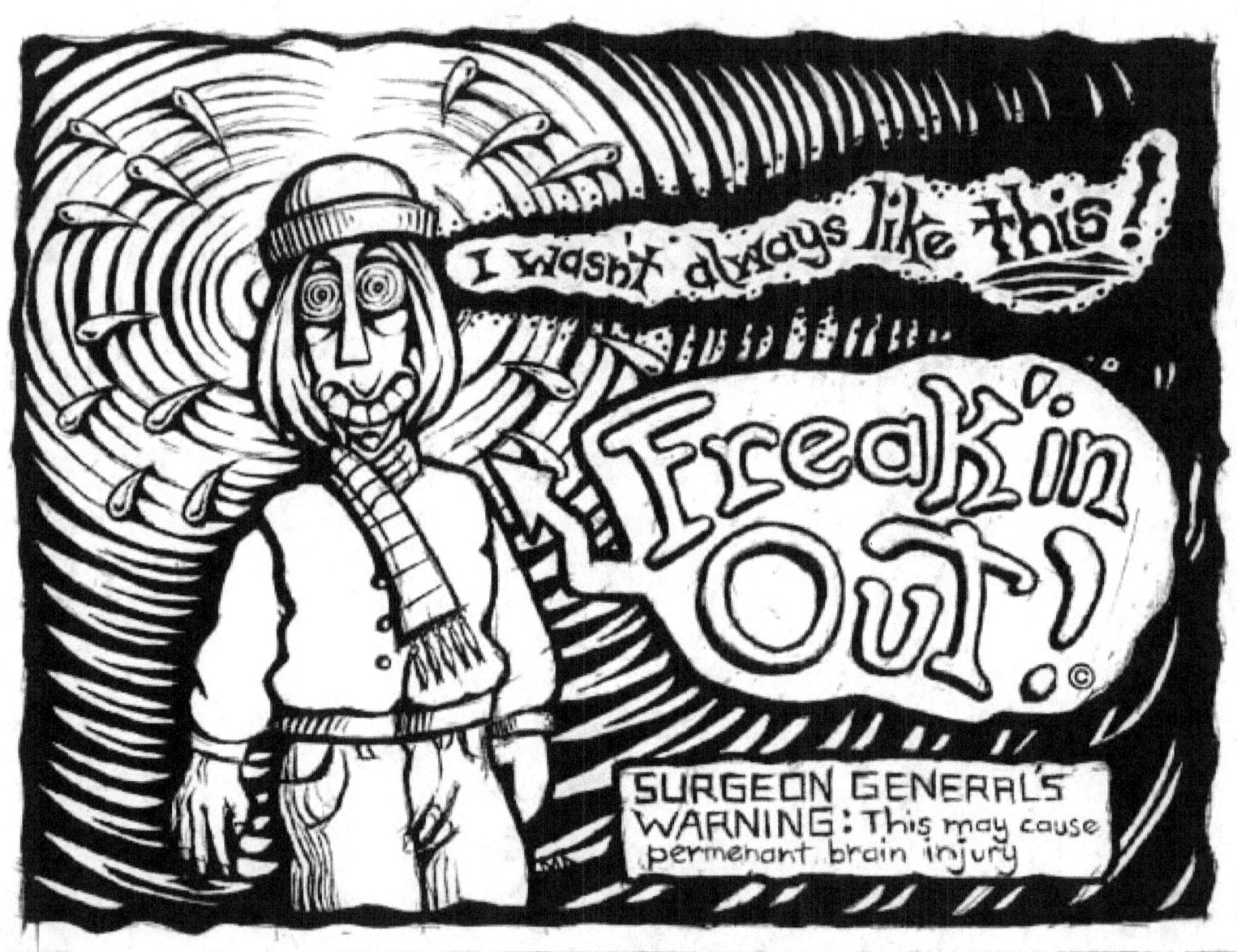

"Freak'in Out"

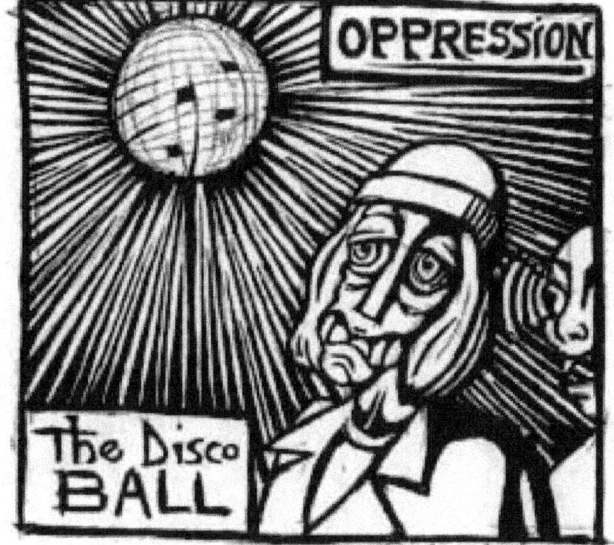

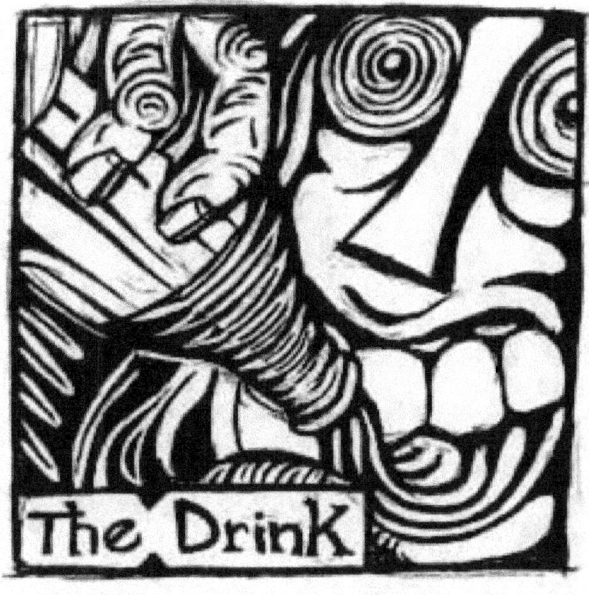

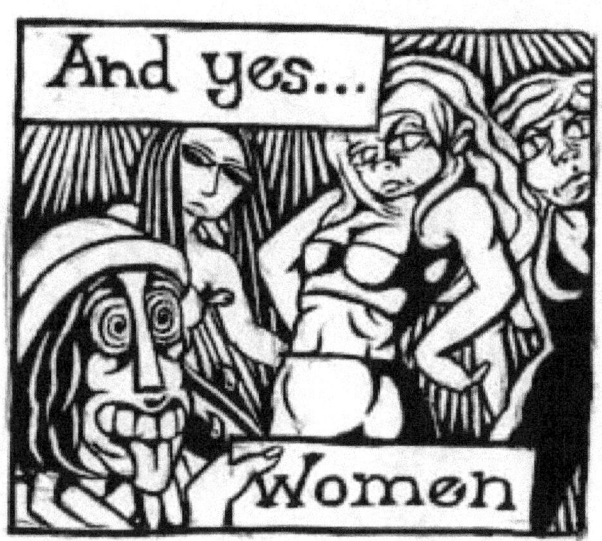

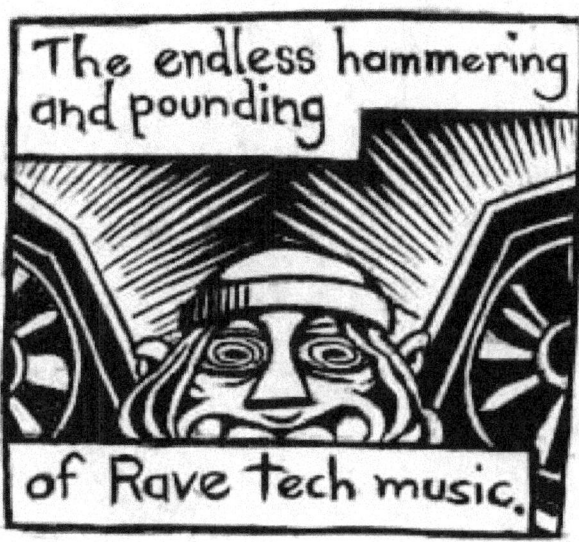

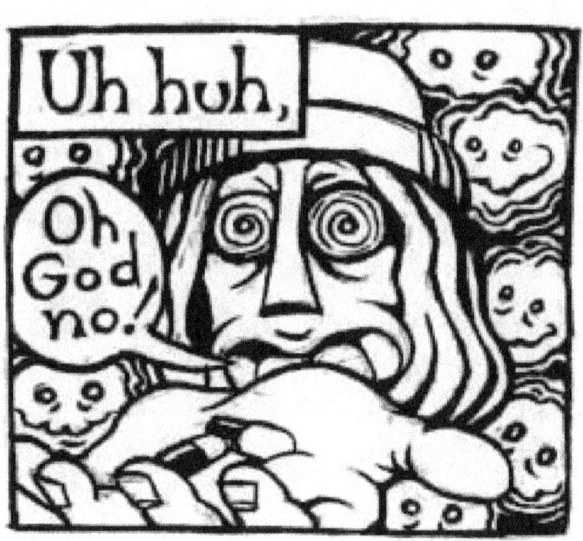

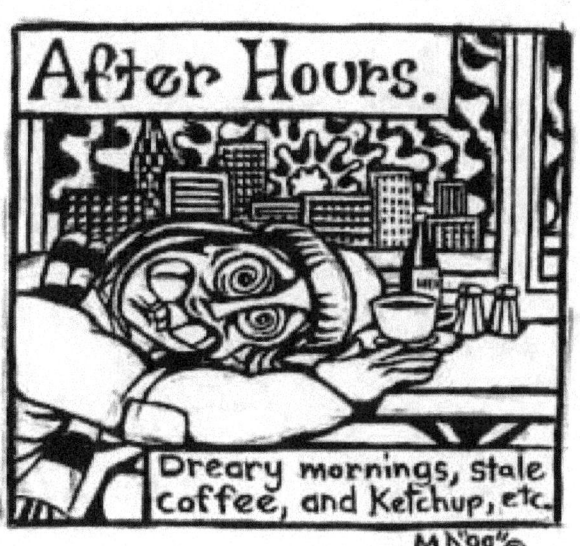

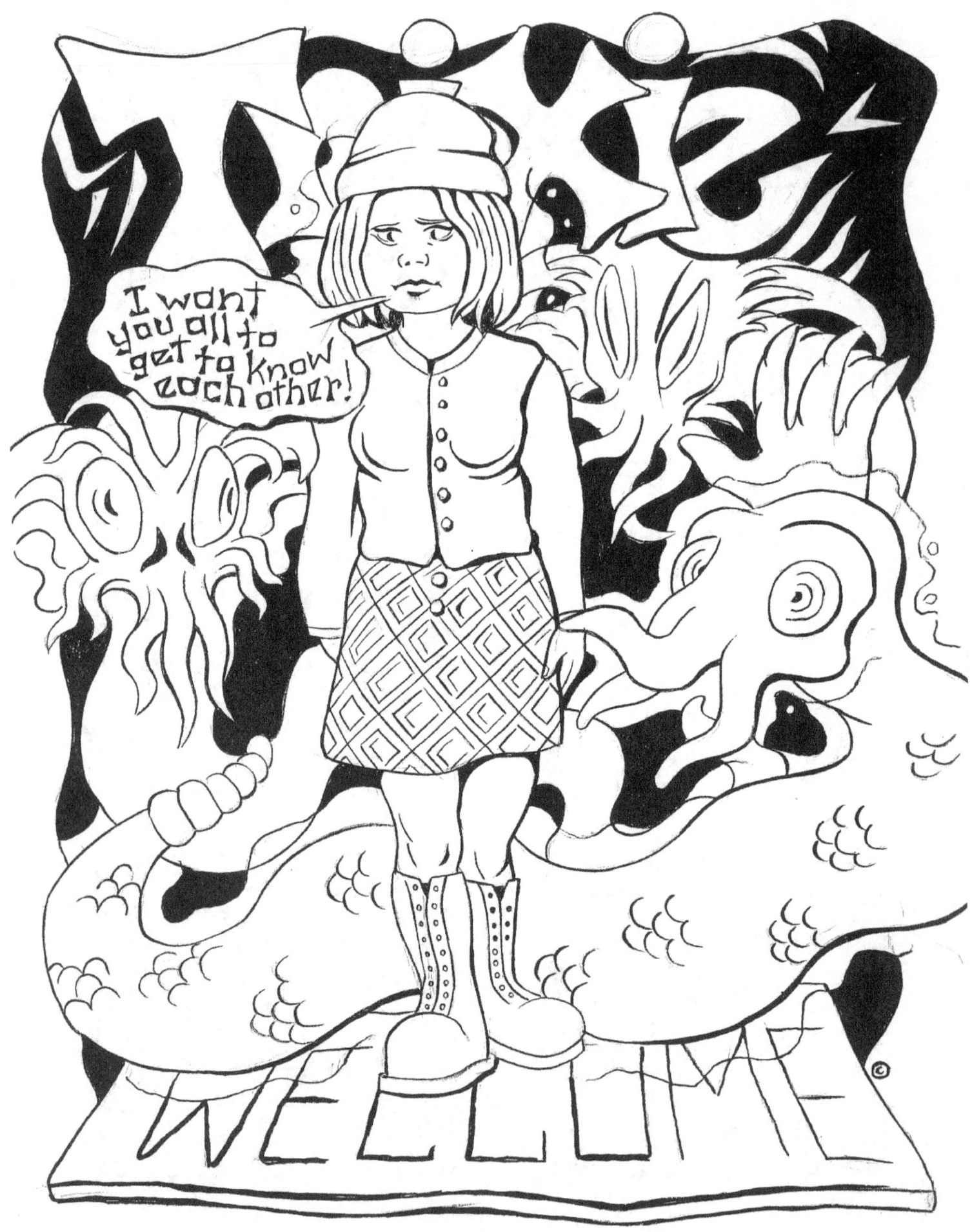

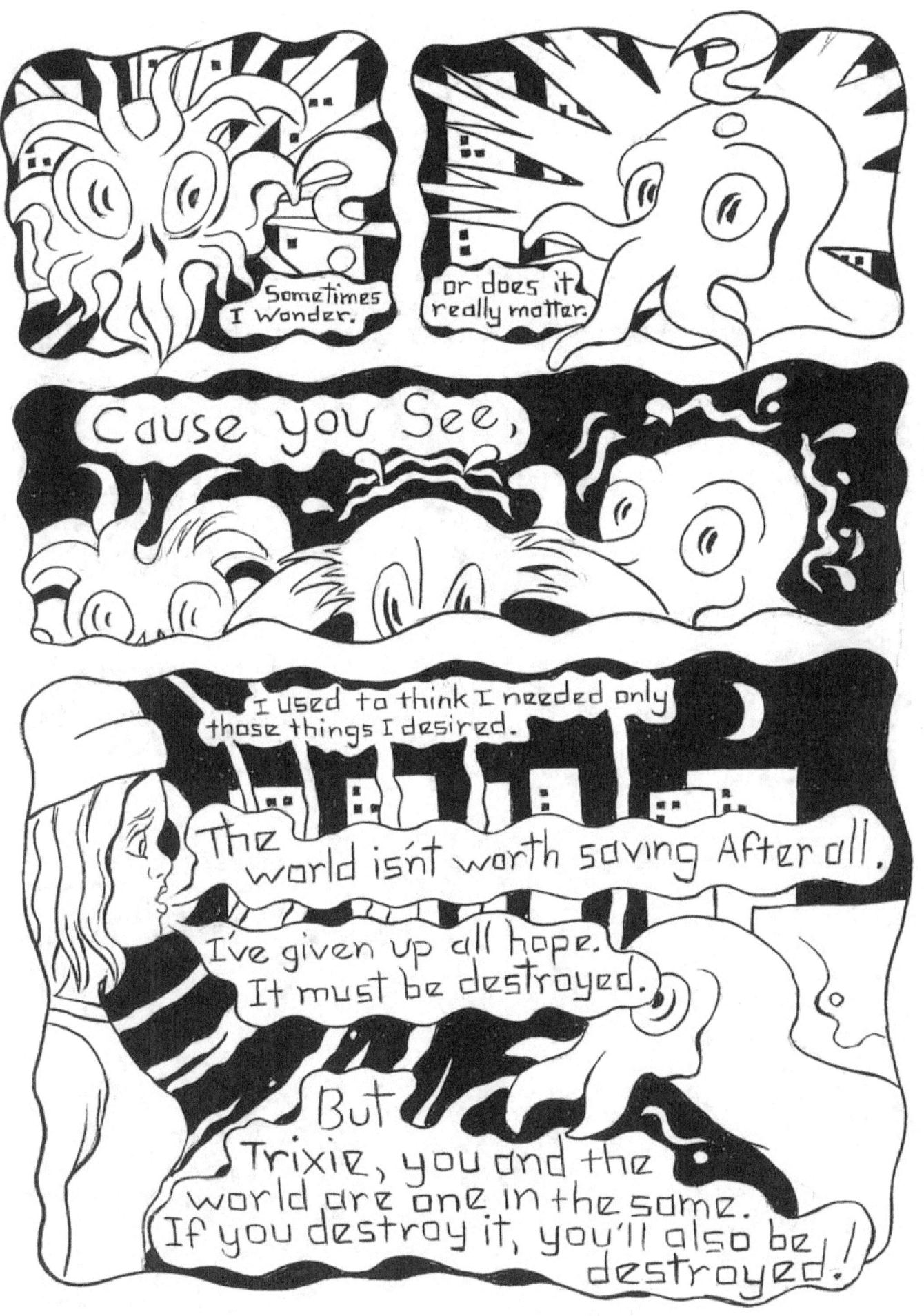

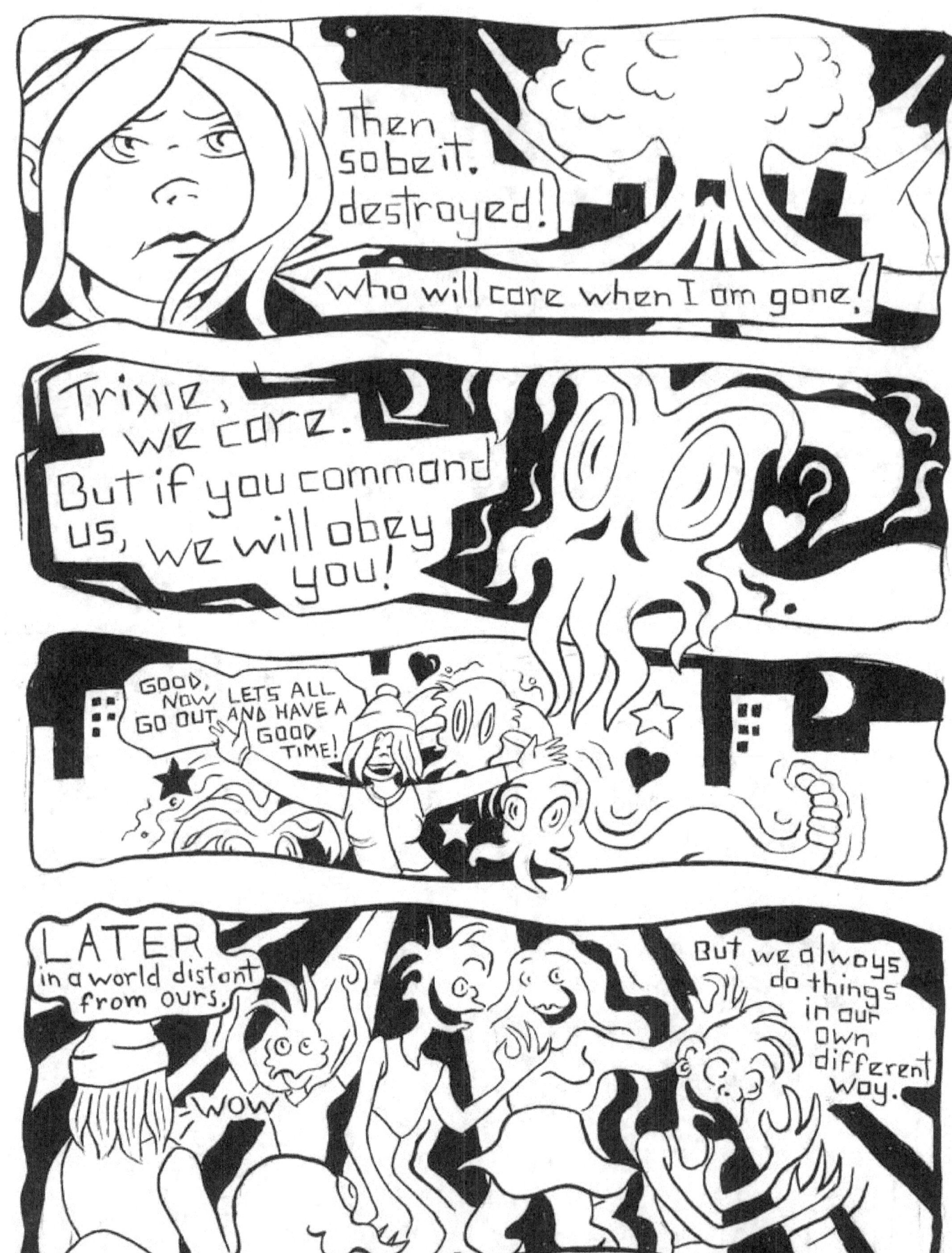

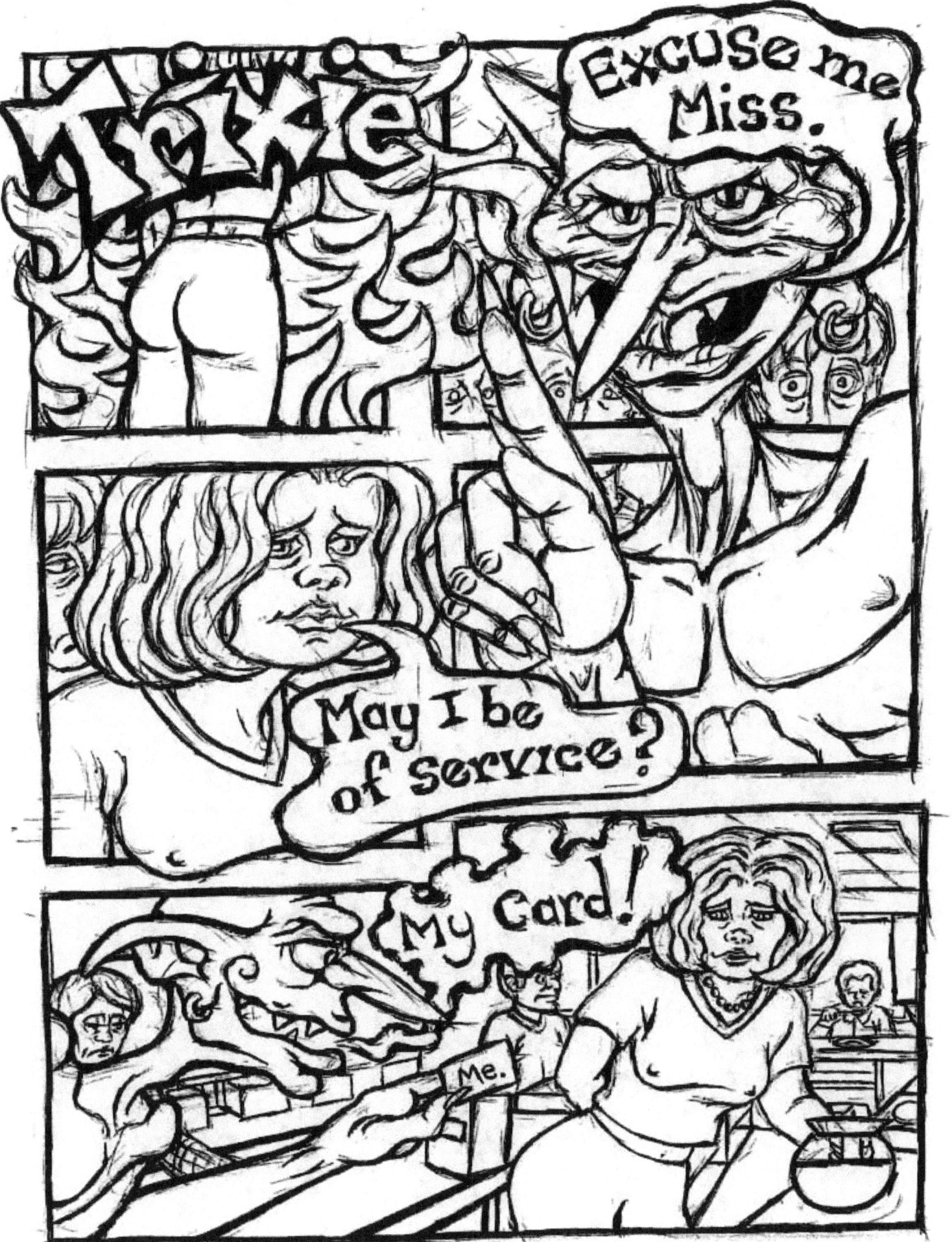

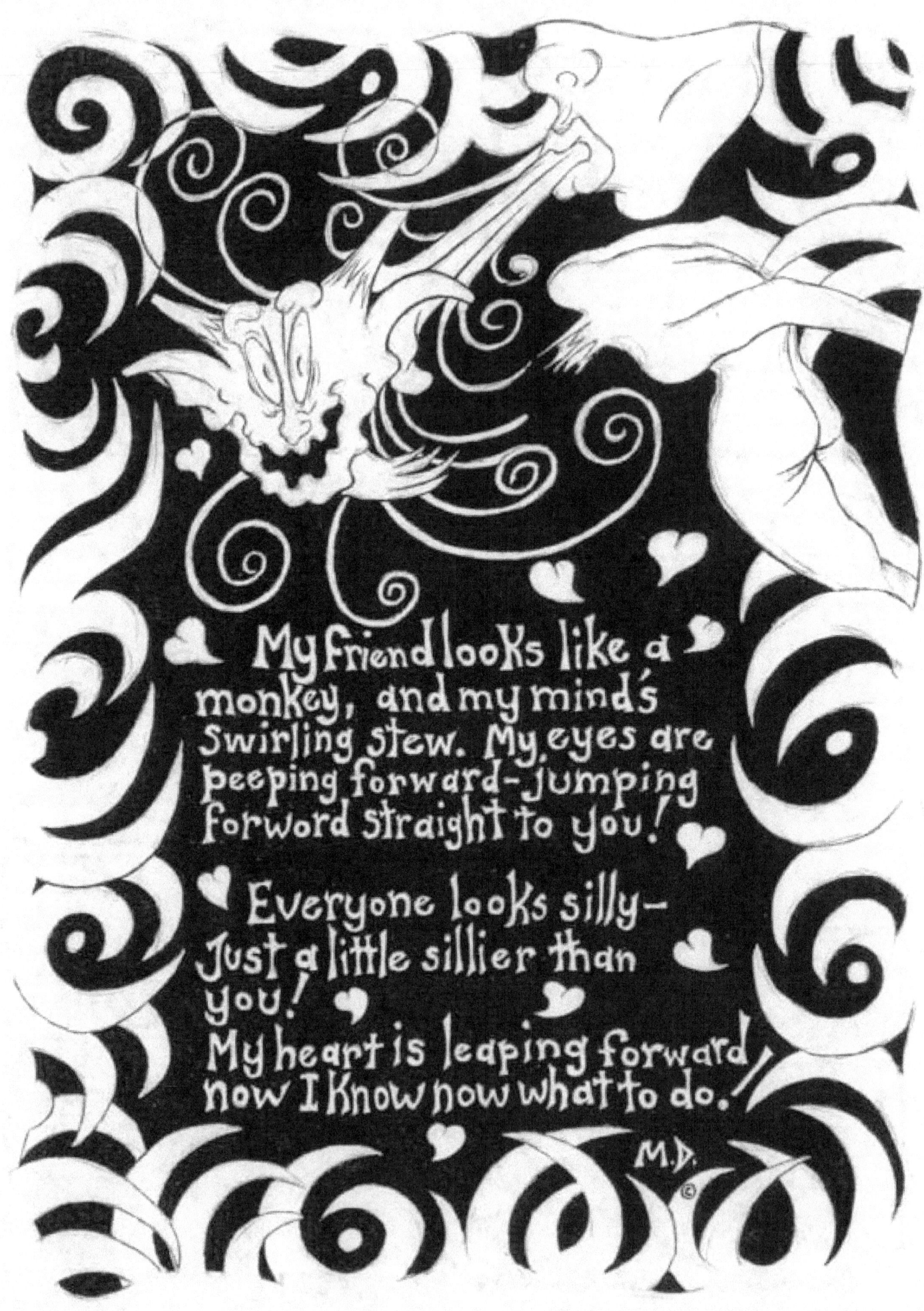

My friend looks like a monkey, and my mind's swirling stew. My eyes are peeping forward-jumping forword straight to you!

Everyone looks silly— Just a little sillier than you!

My heart is leaping forward now I know now what to do.!

M.D.

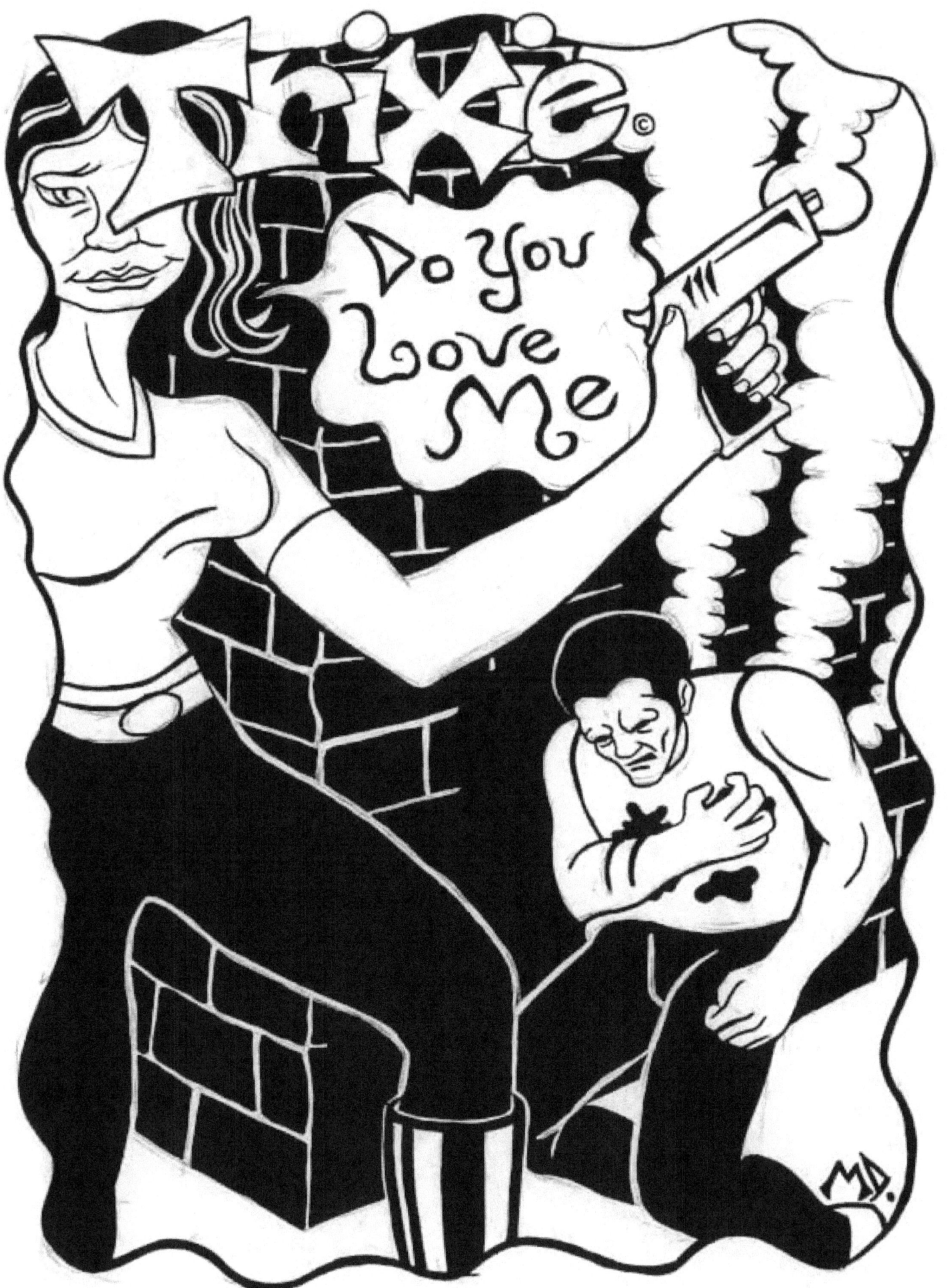

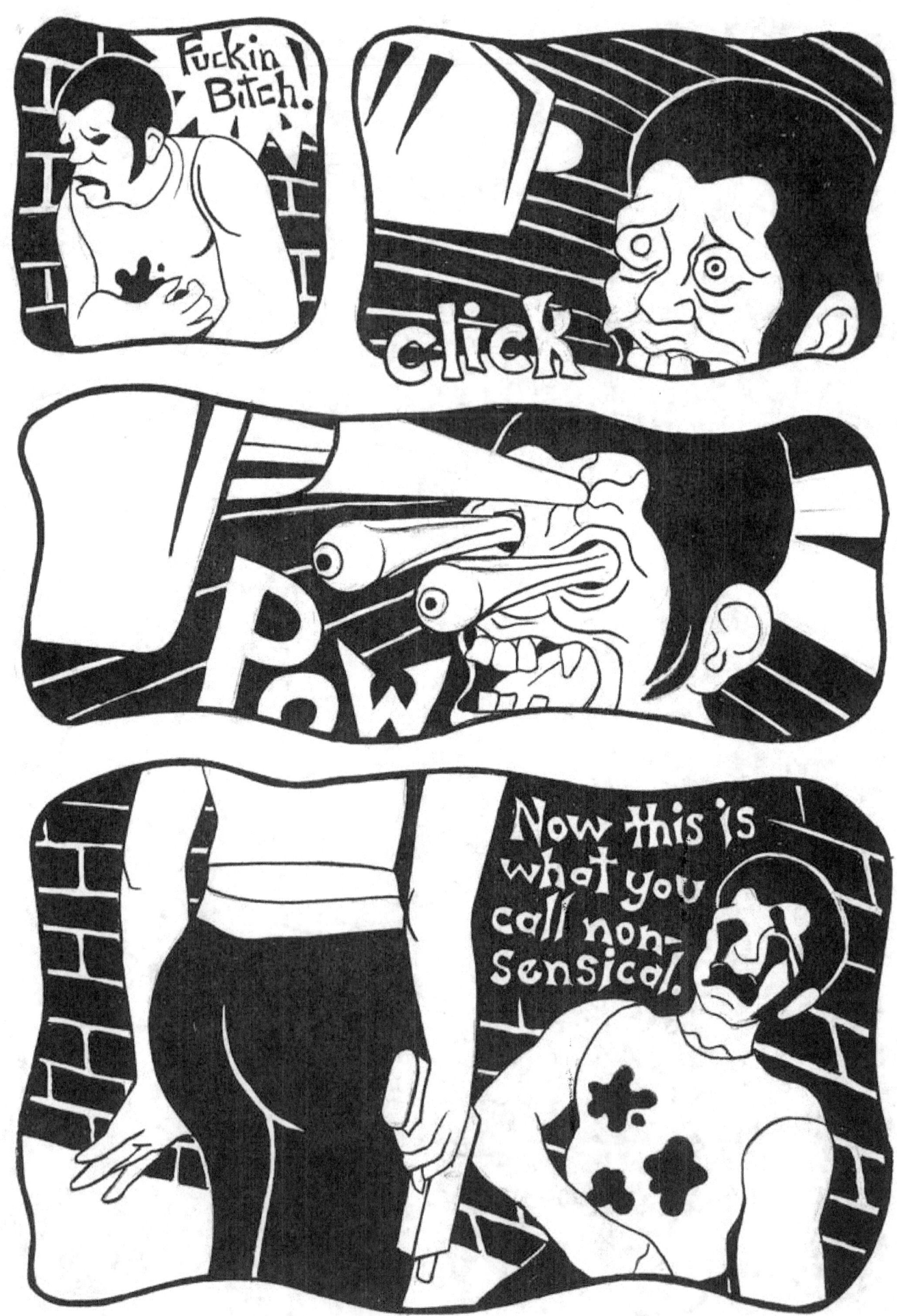

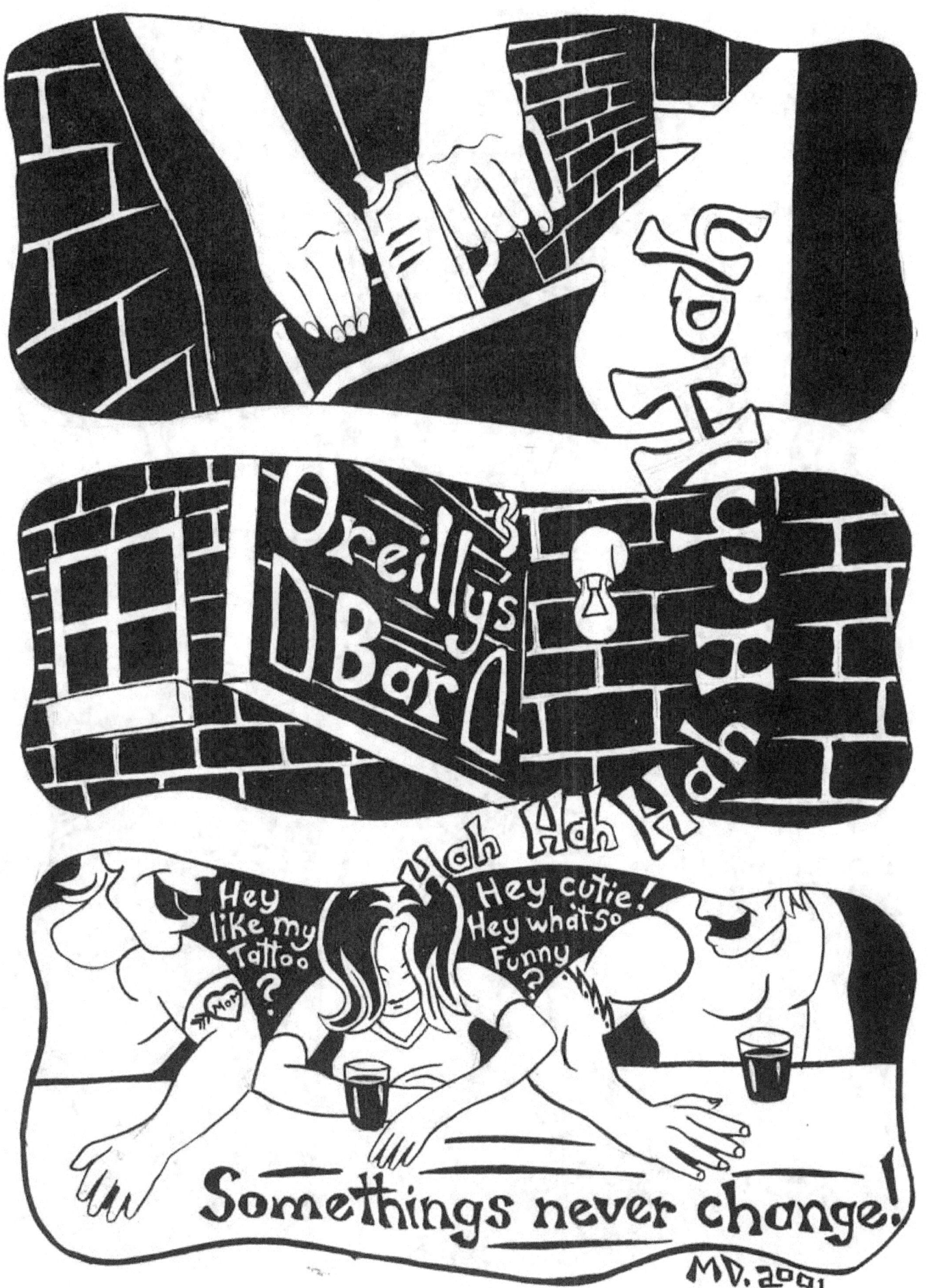

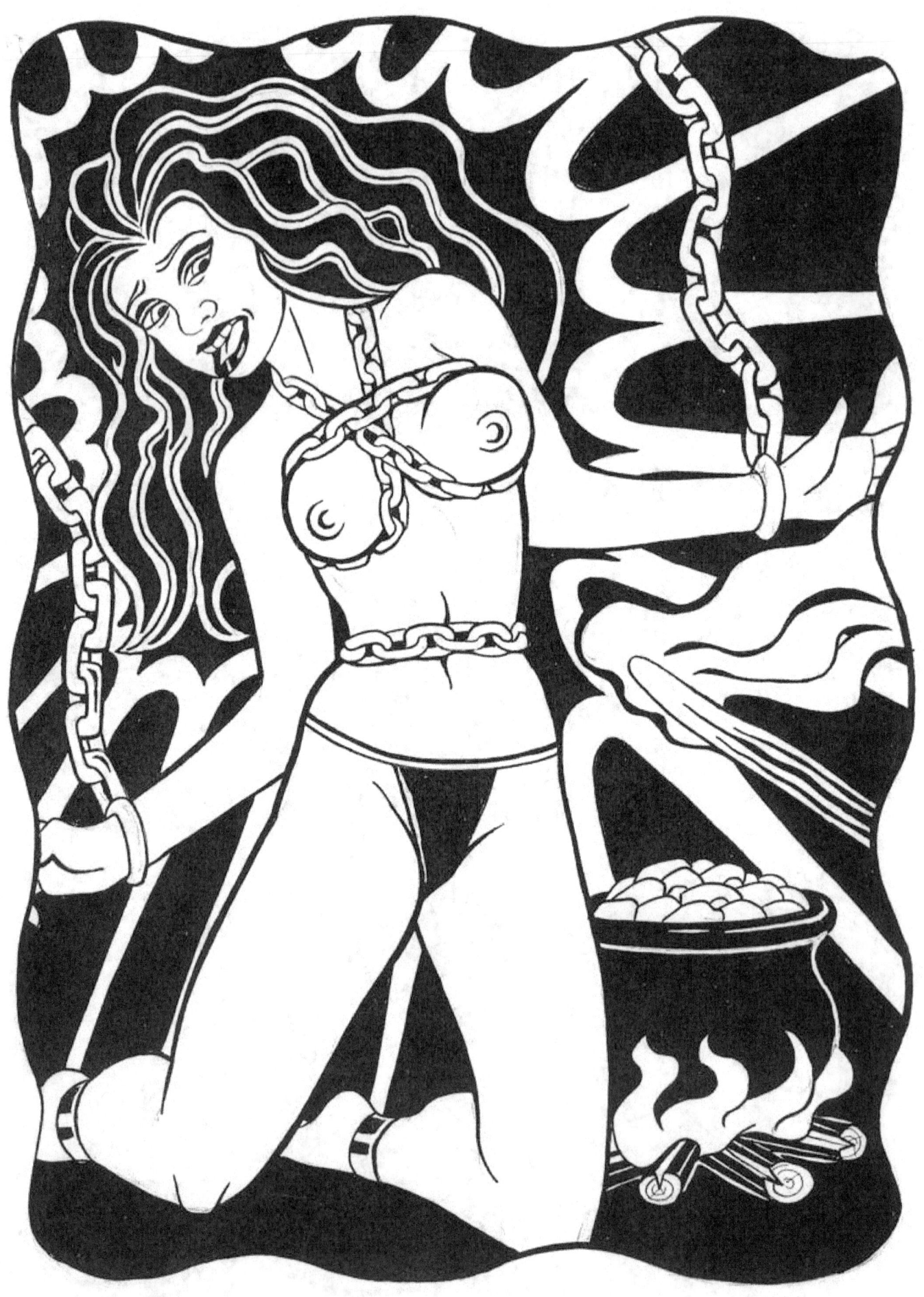

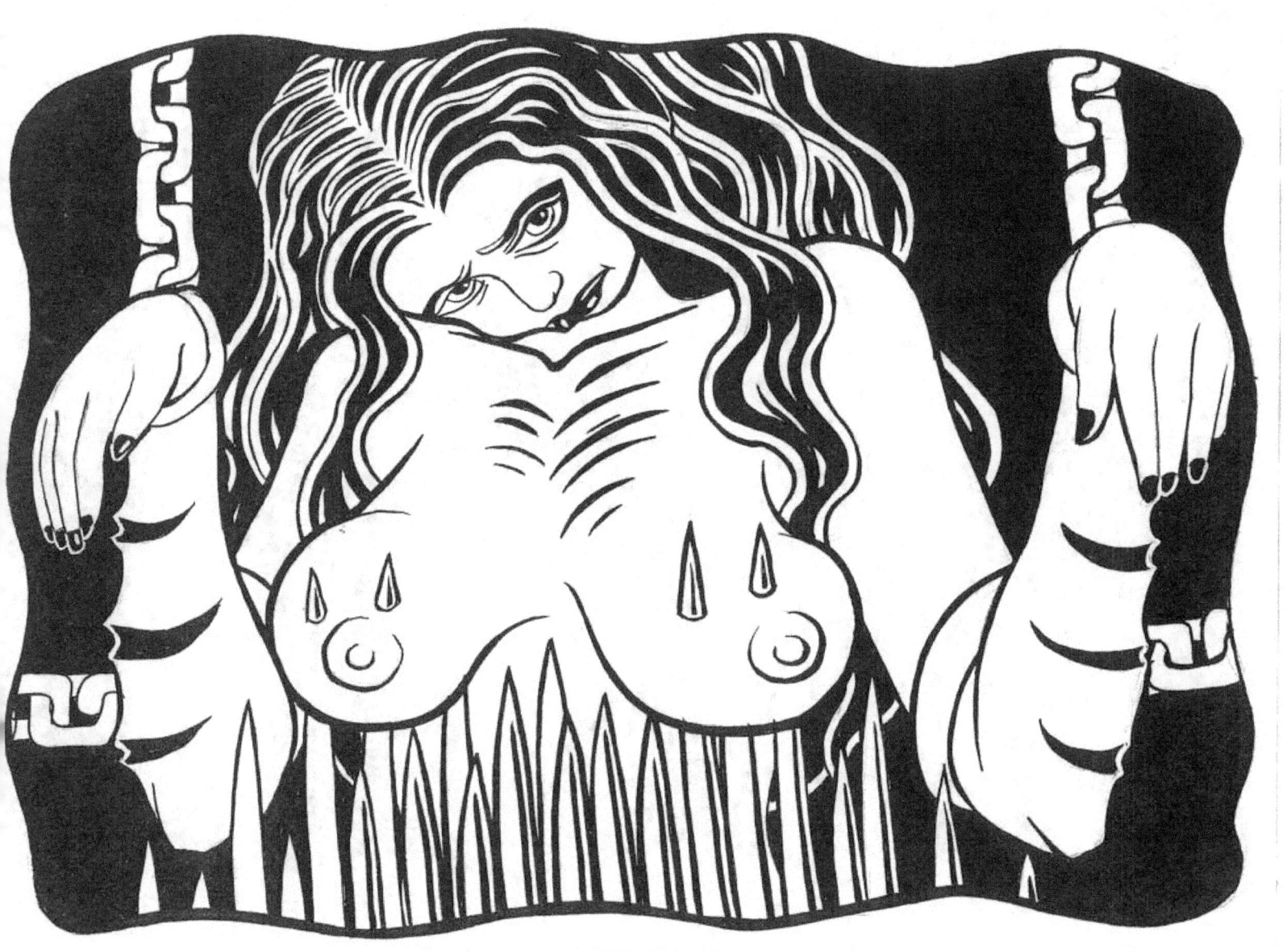

"Bondage"
"Spikes"

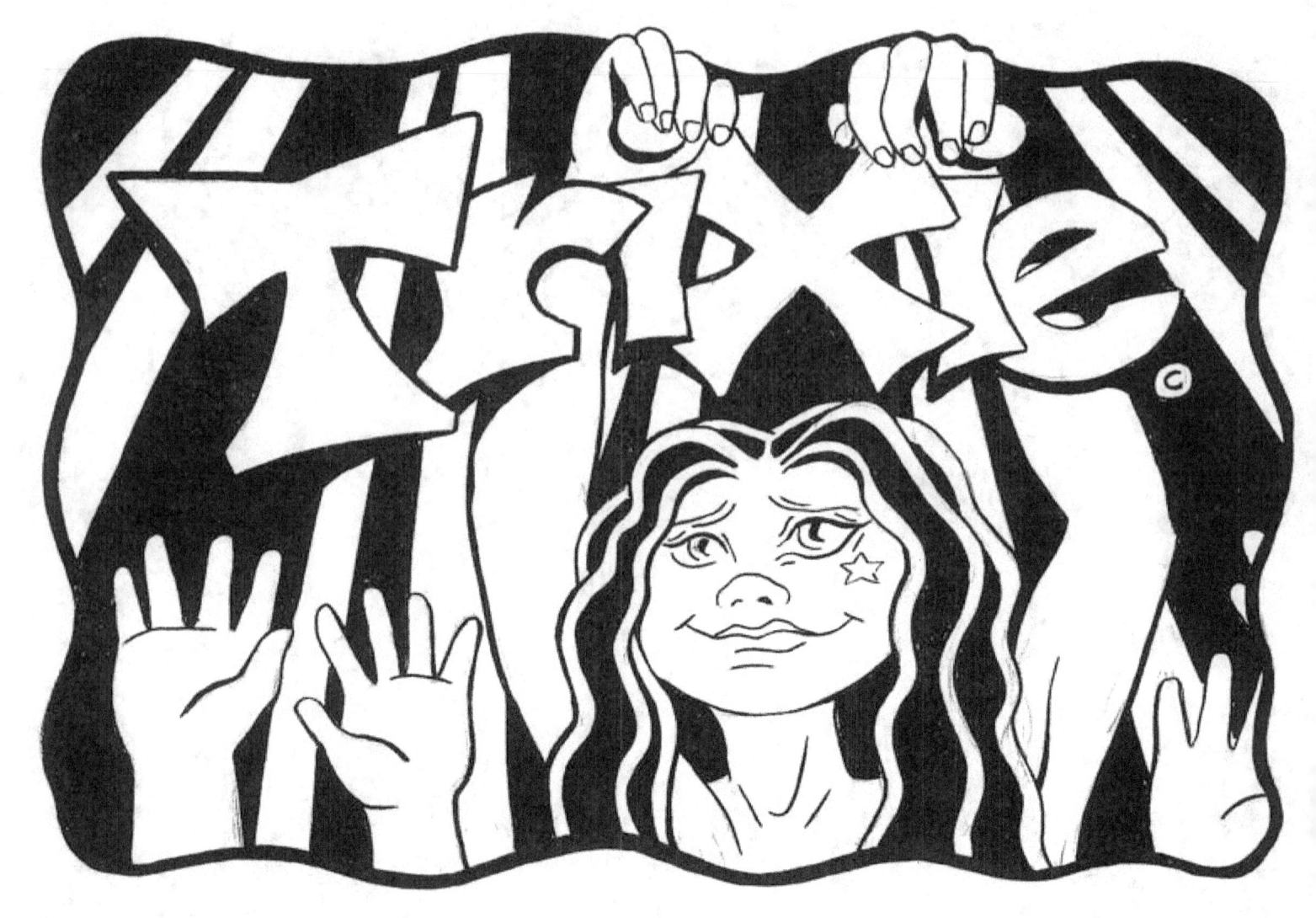

"TRIXIE"

"PRETTY IN THE PLACE TO BE"

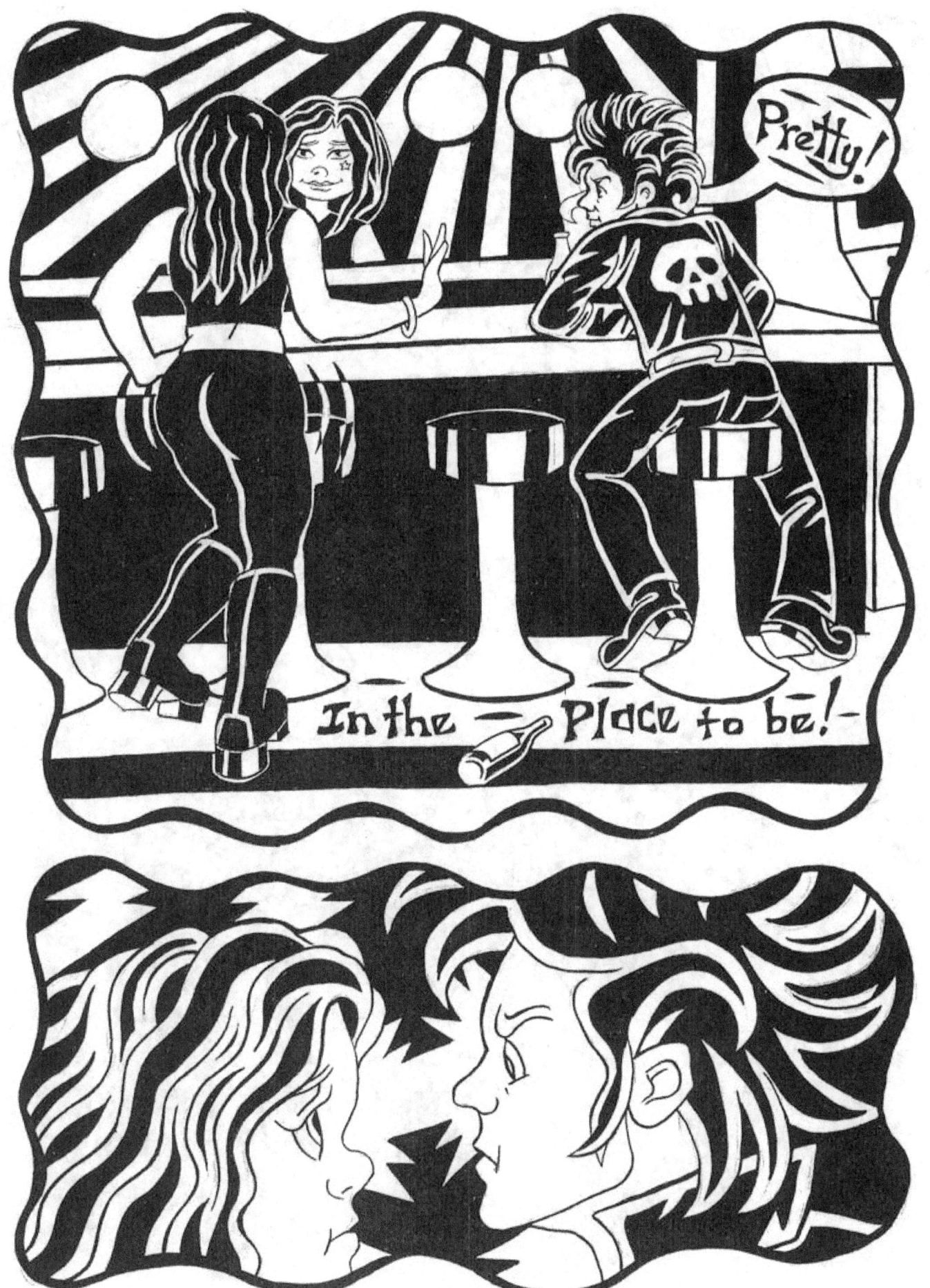

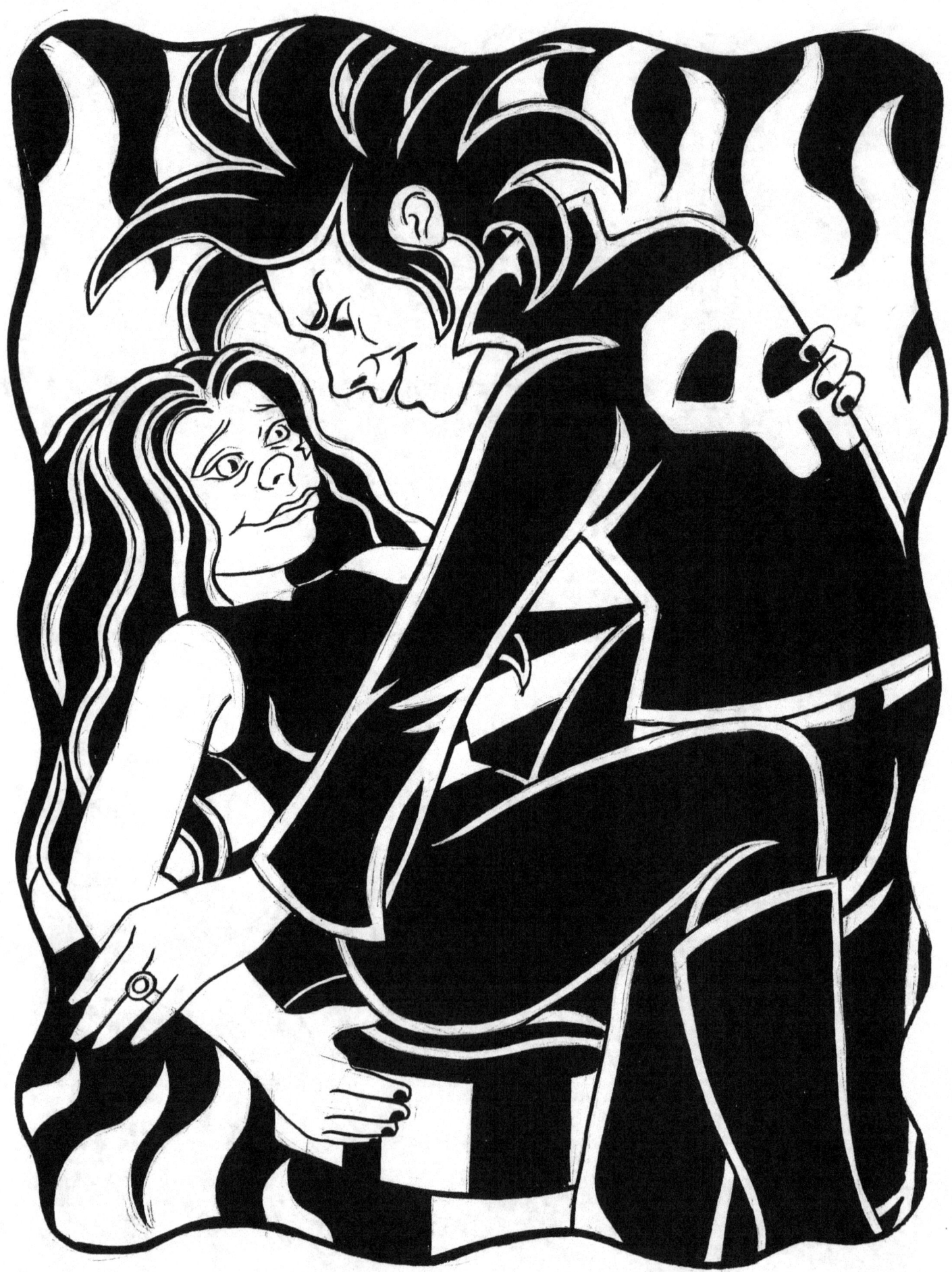

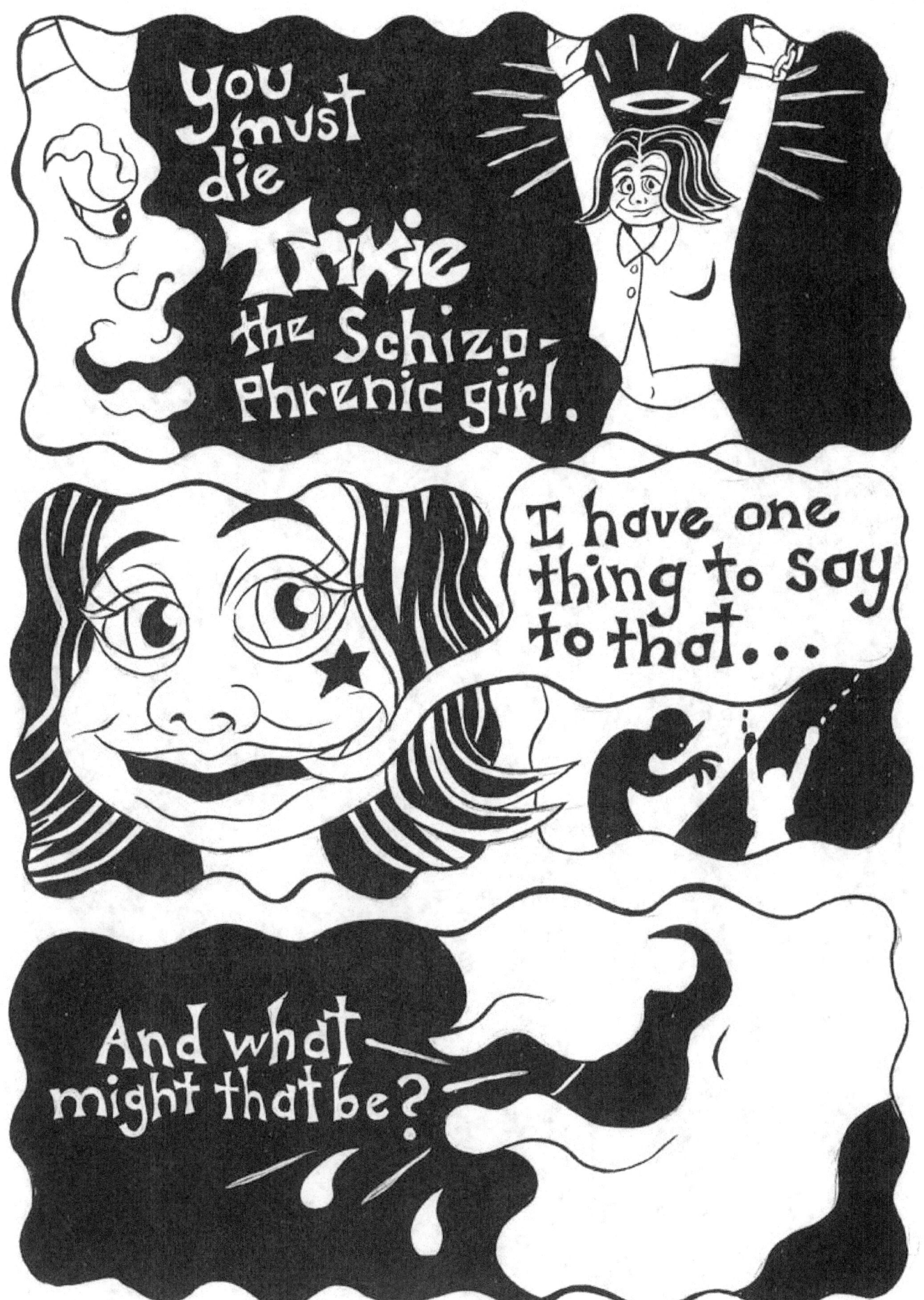

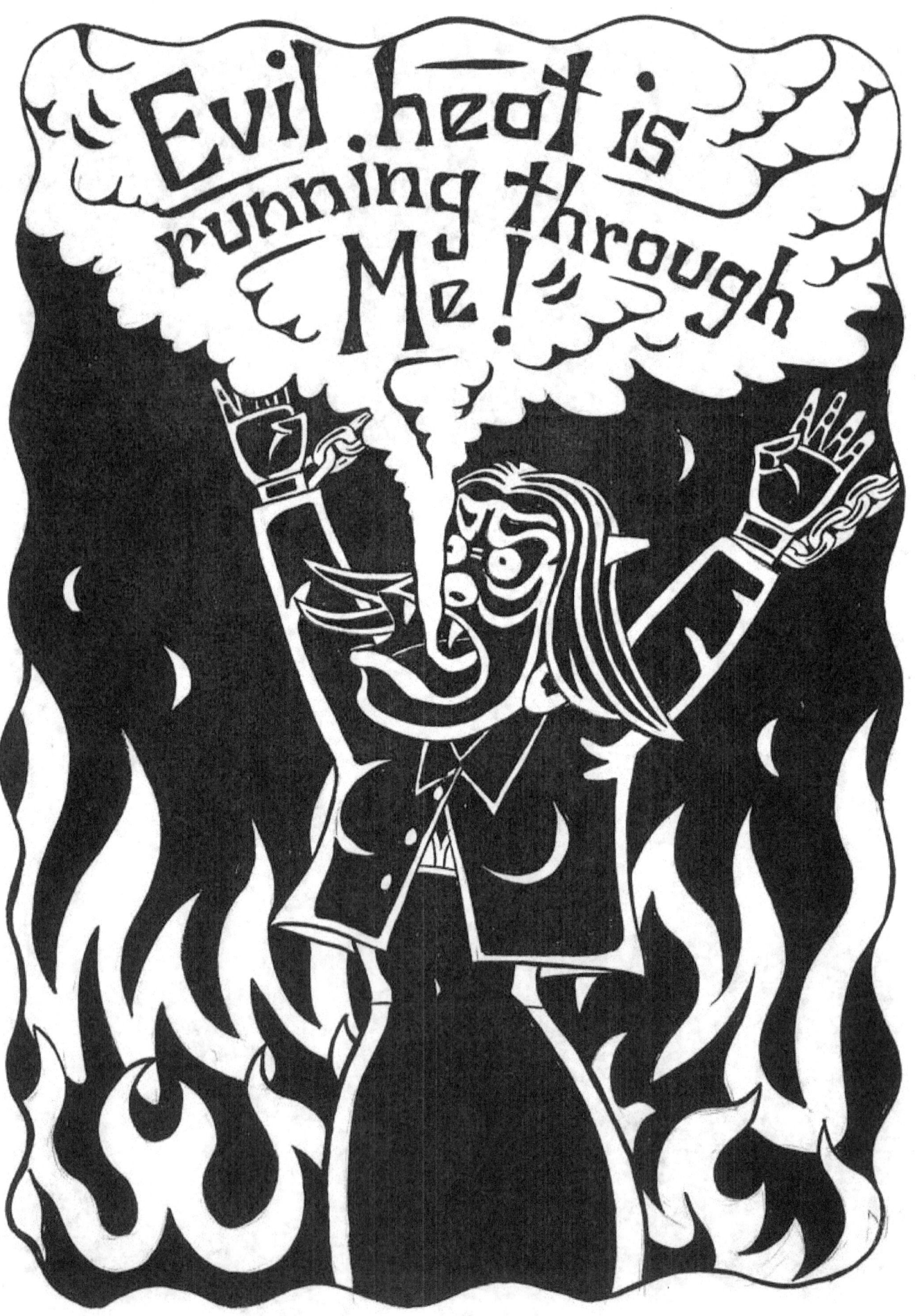

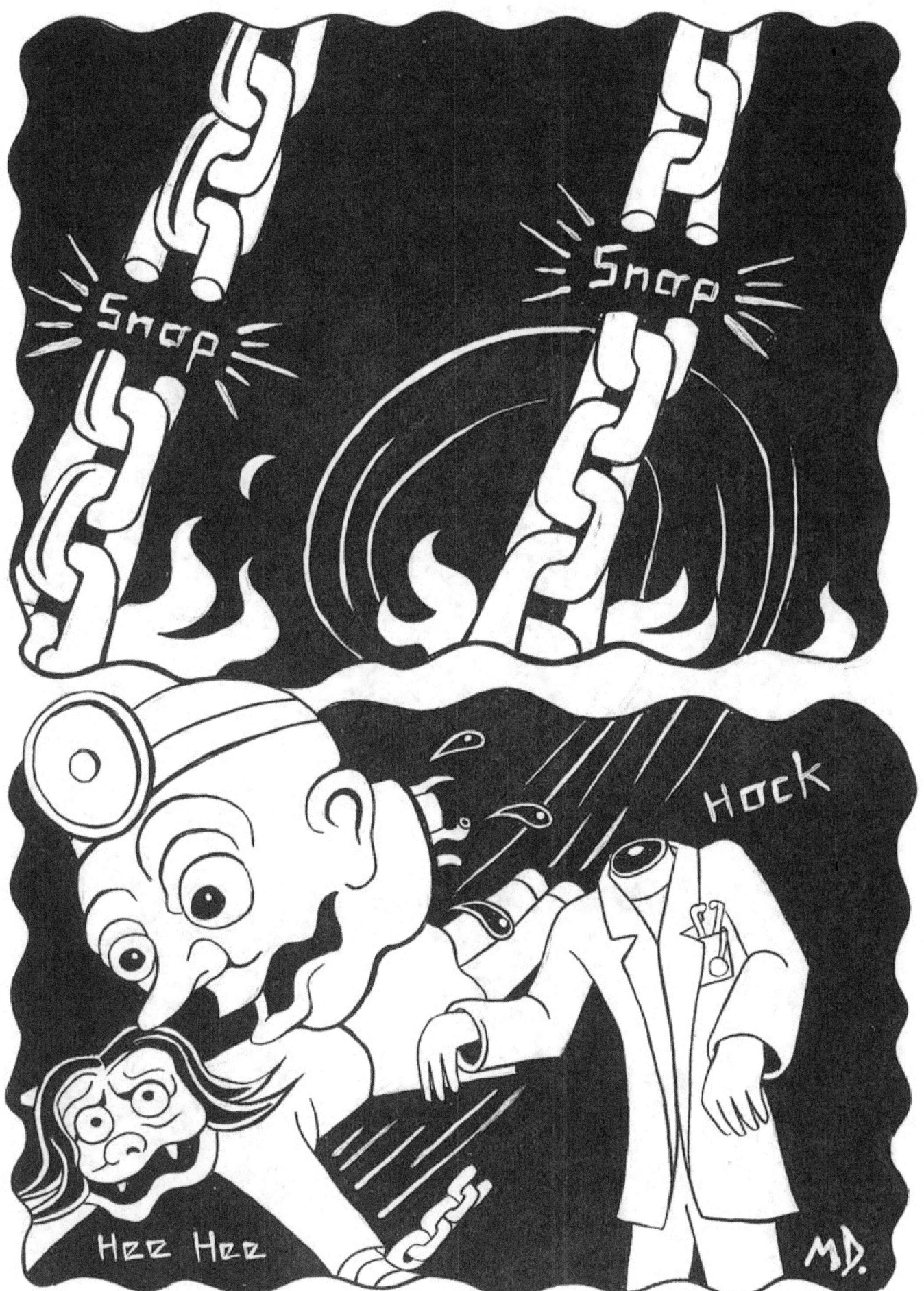

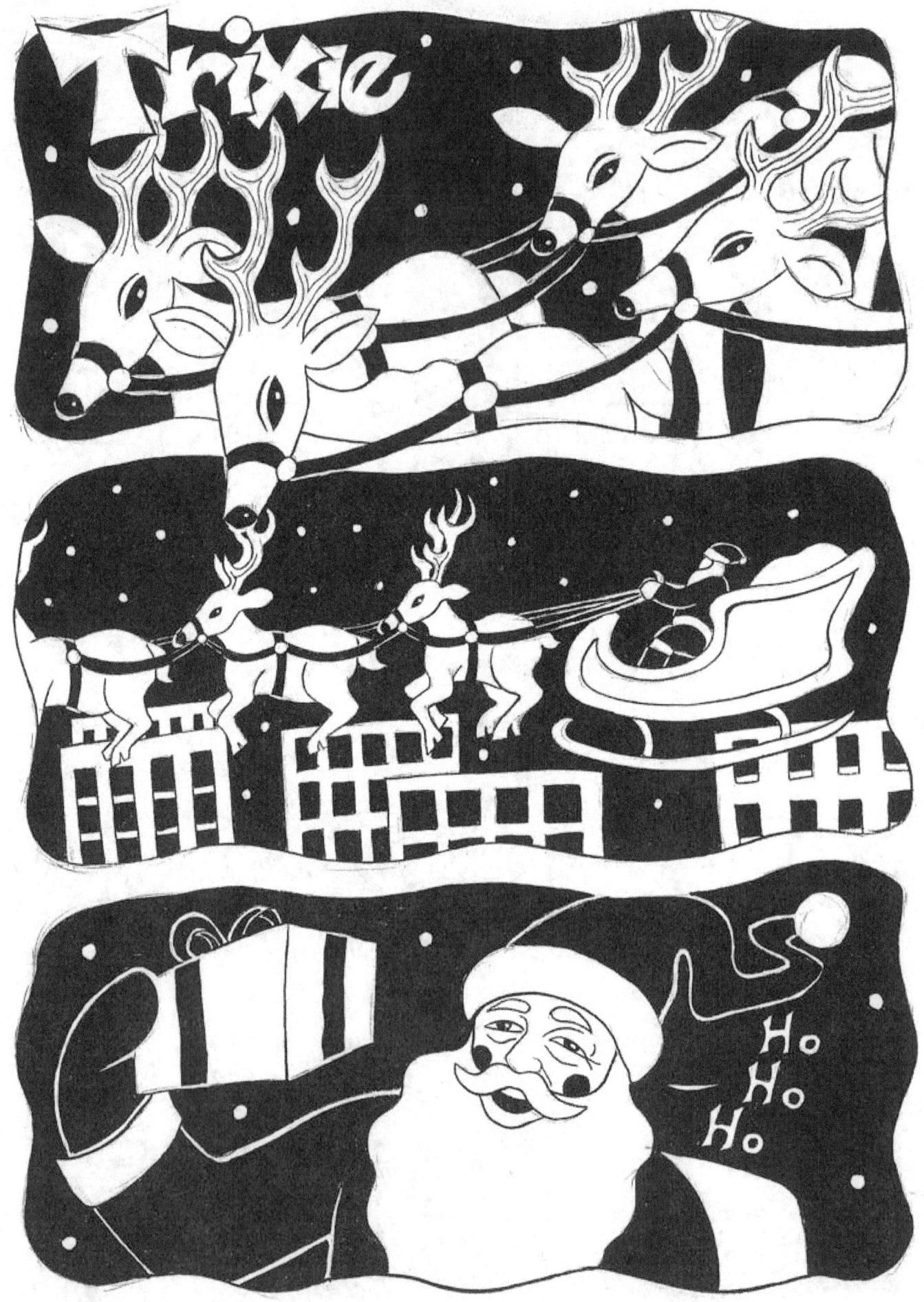

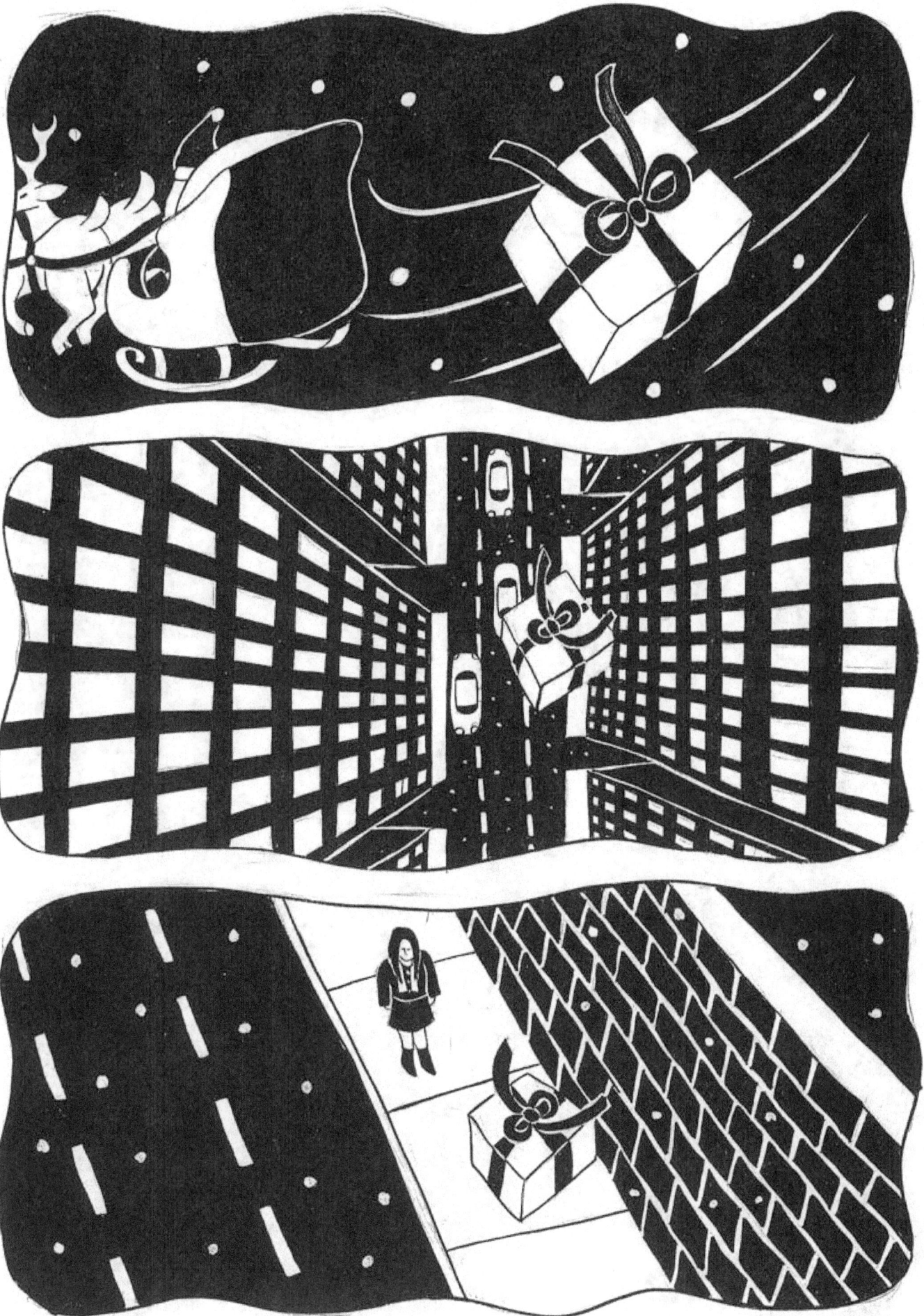

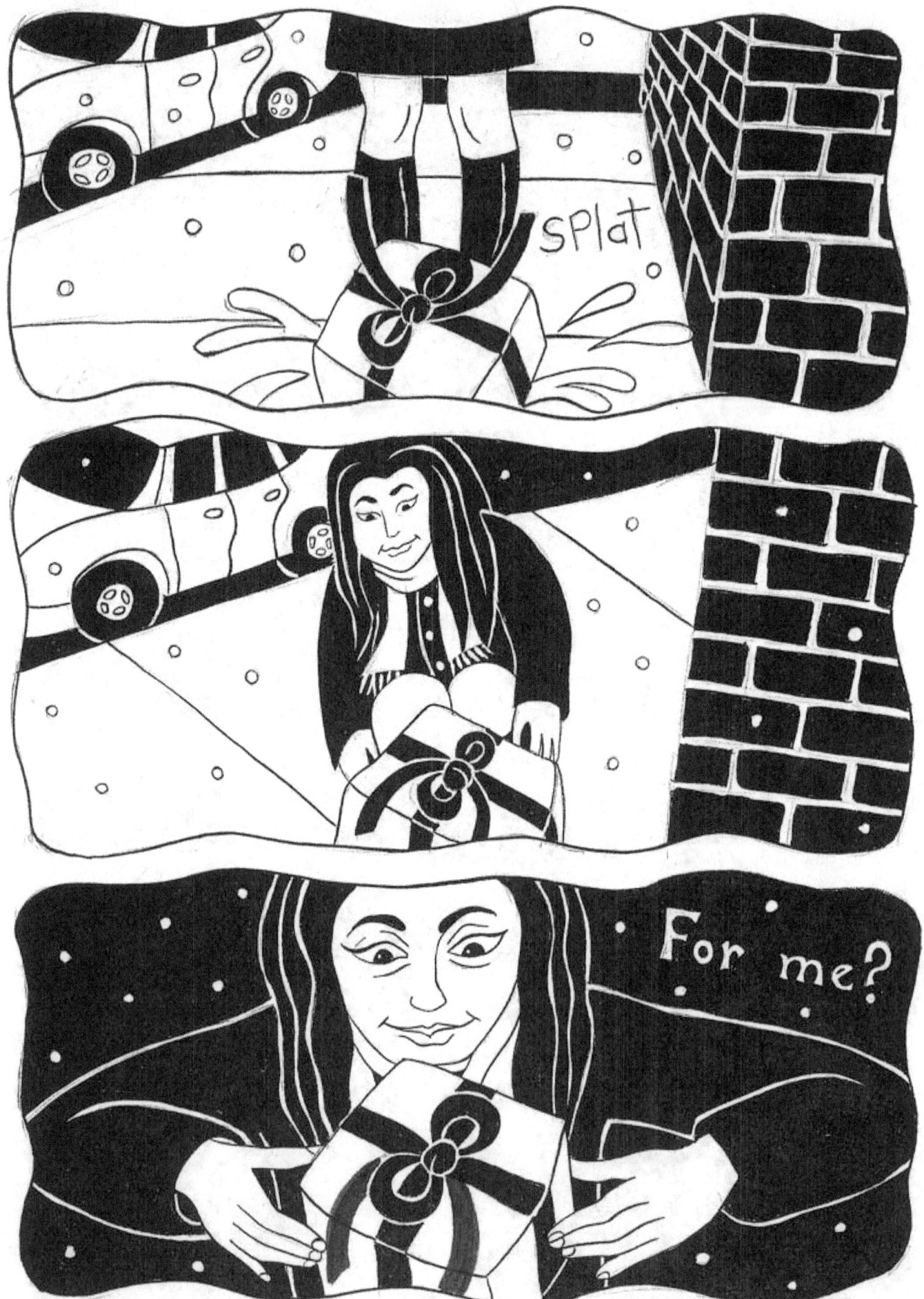

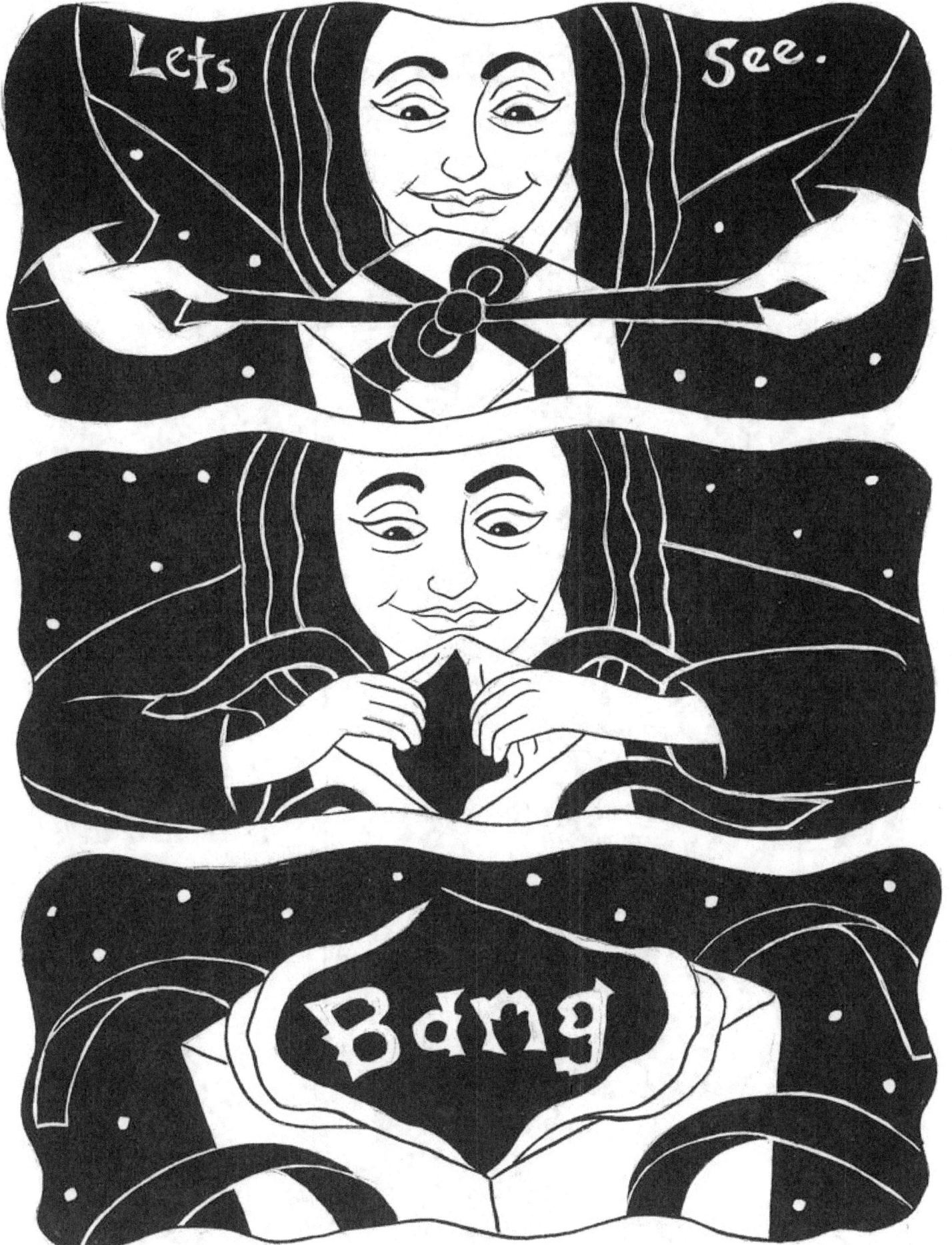

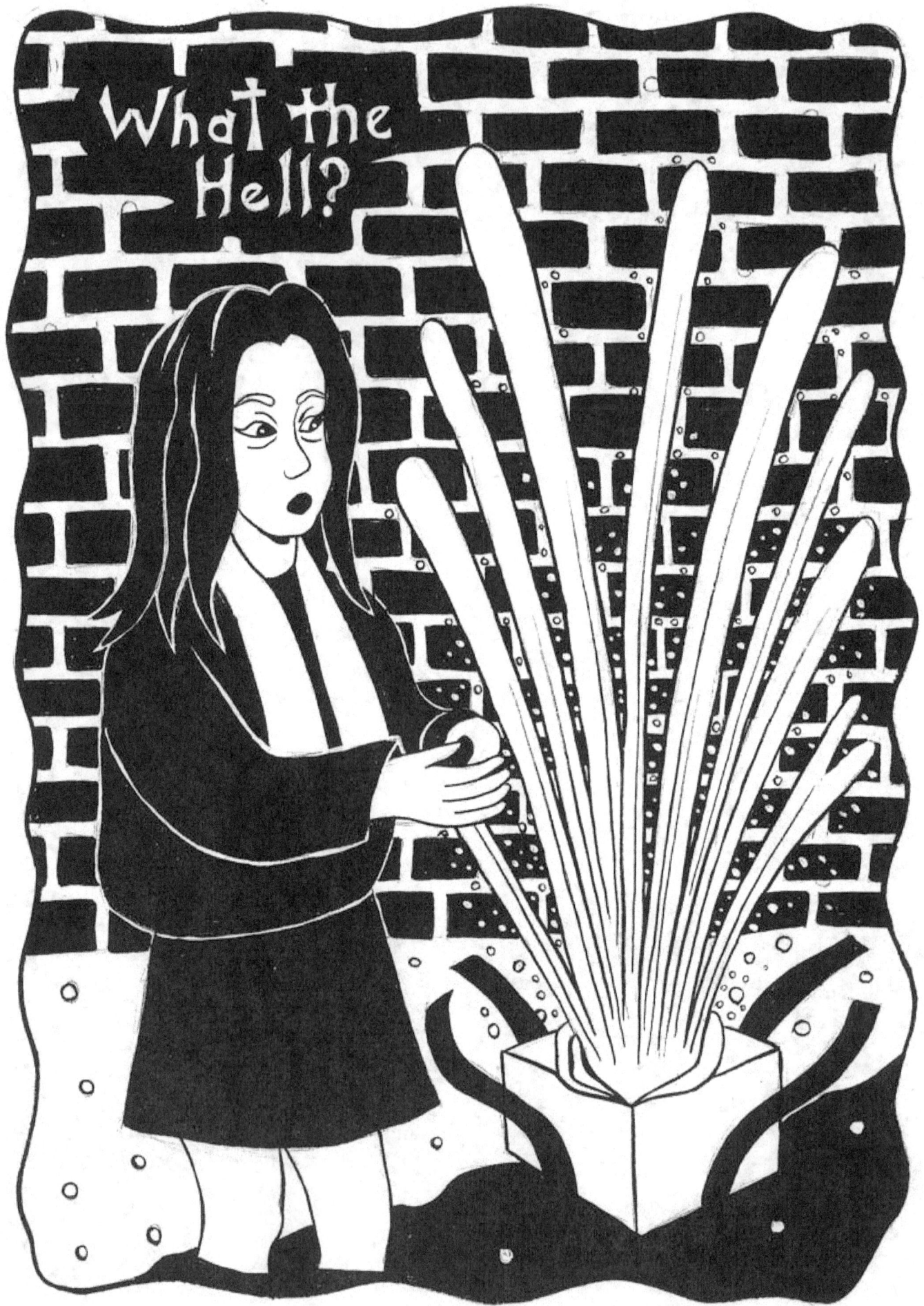

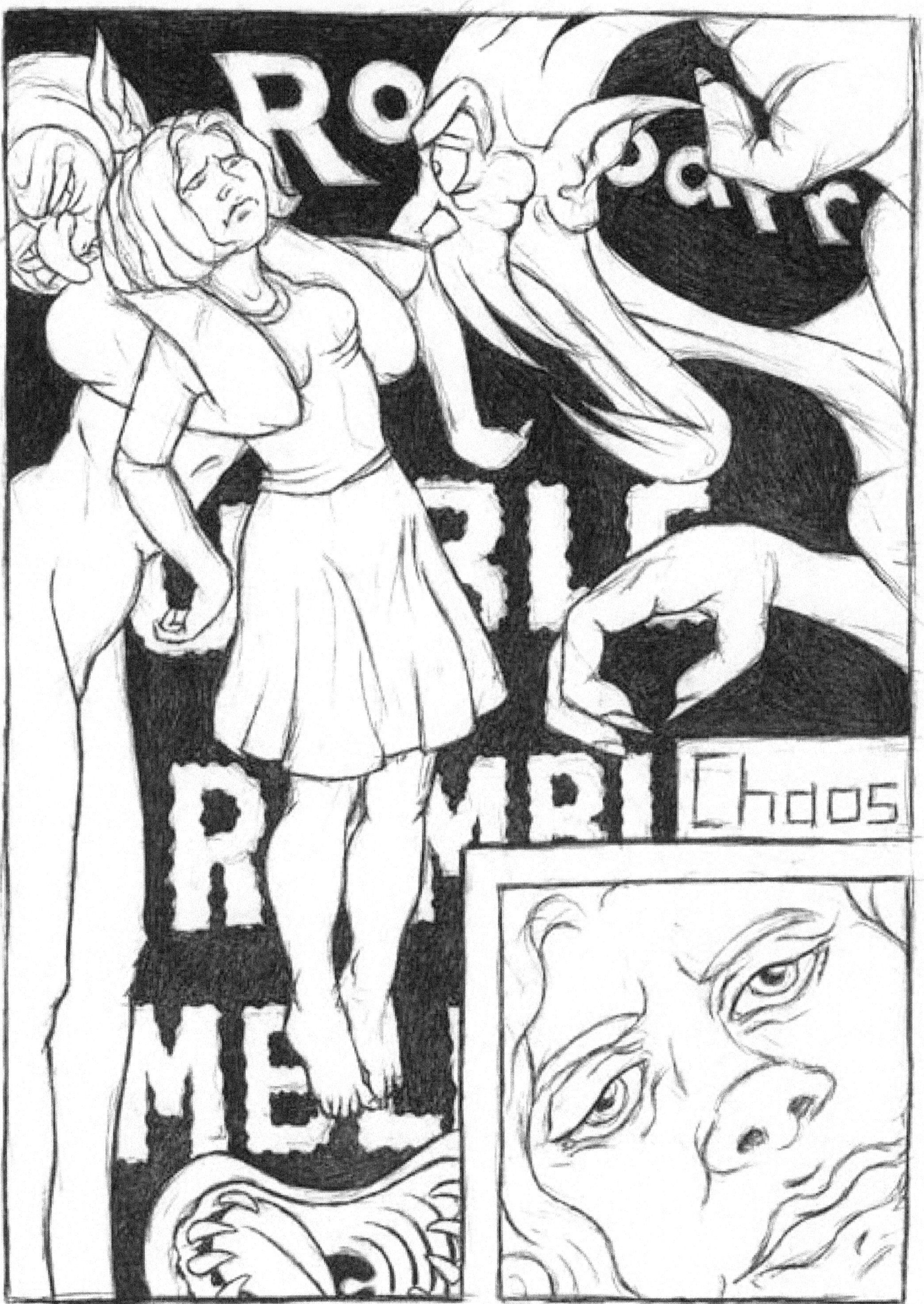

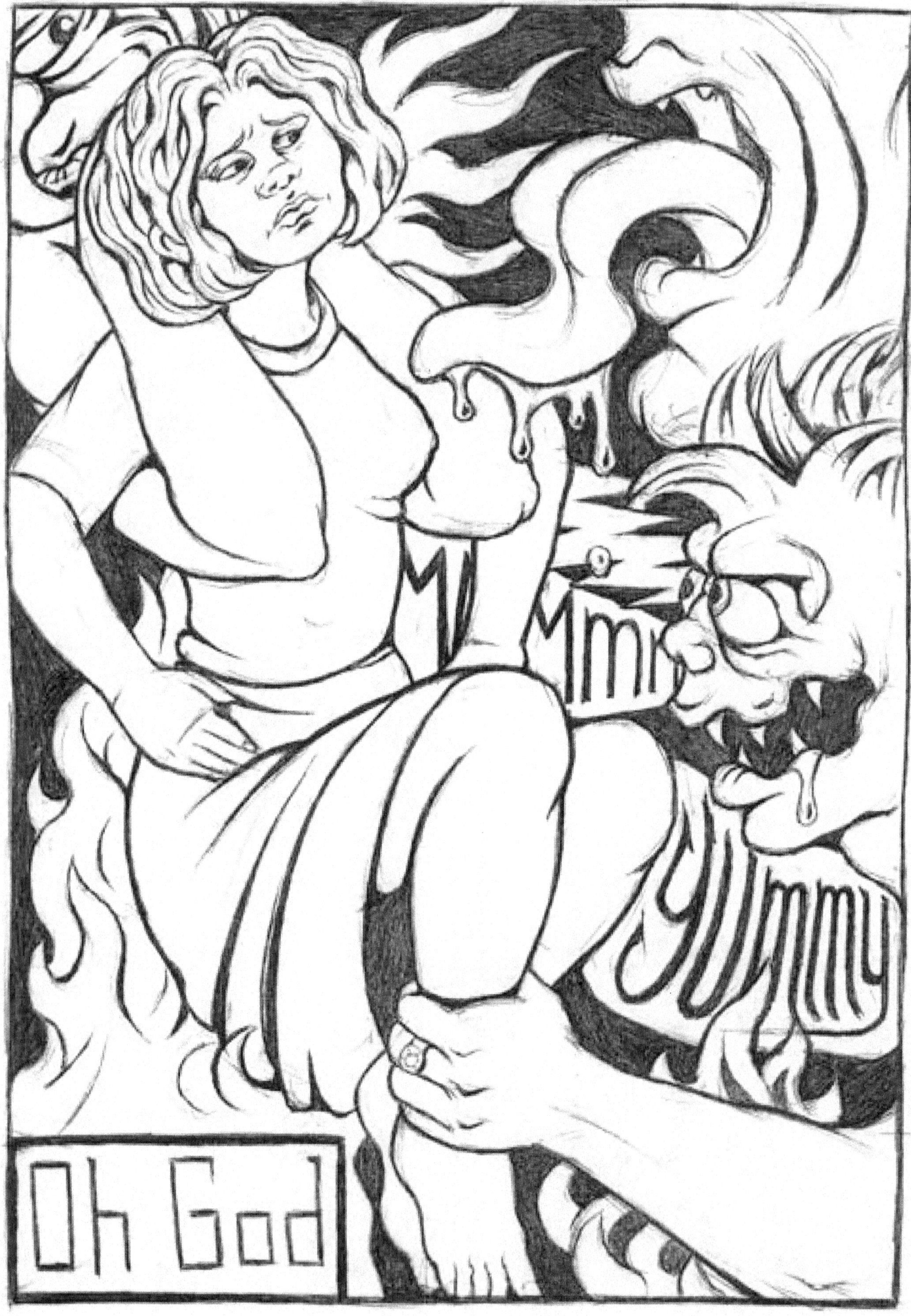

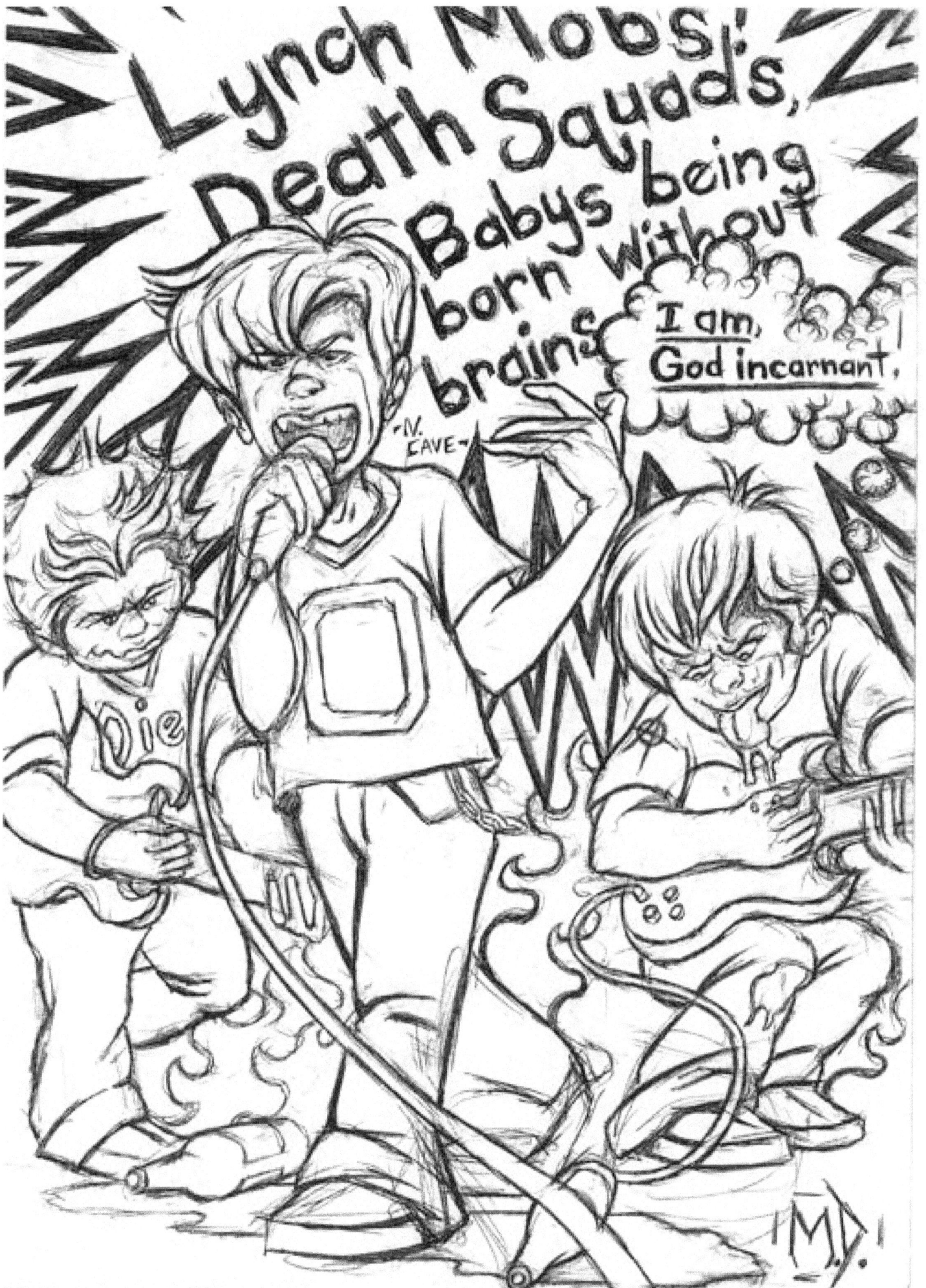

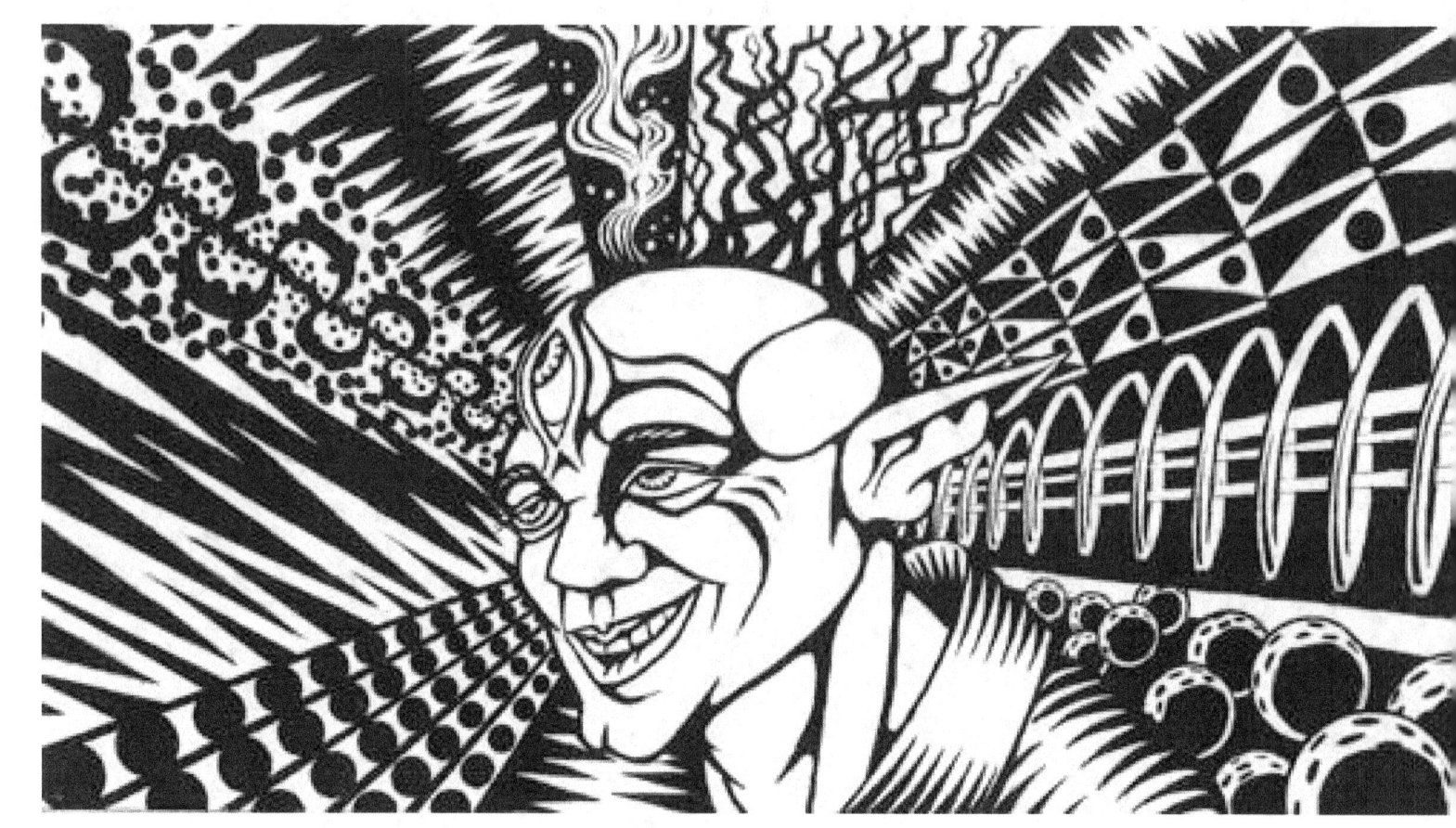

"Psychodelic Troll"

"''Trip you ass off"!!!!

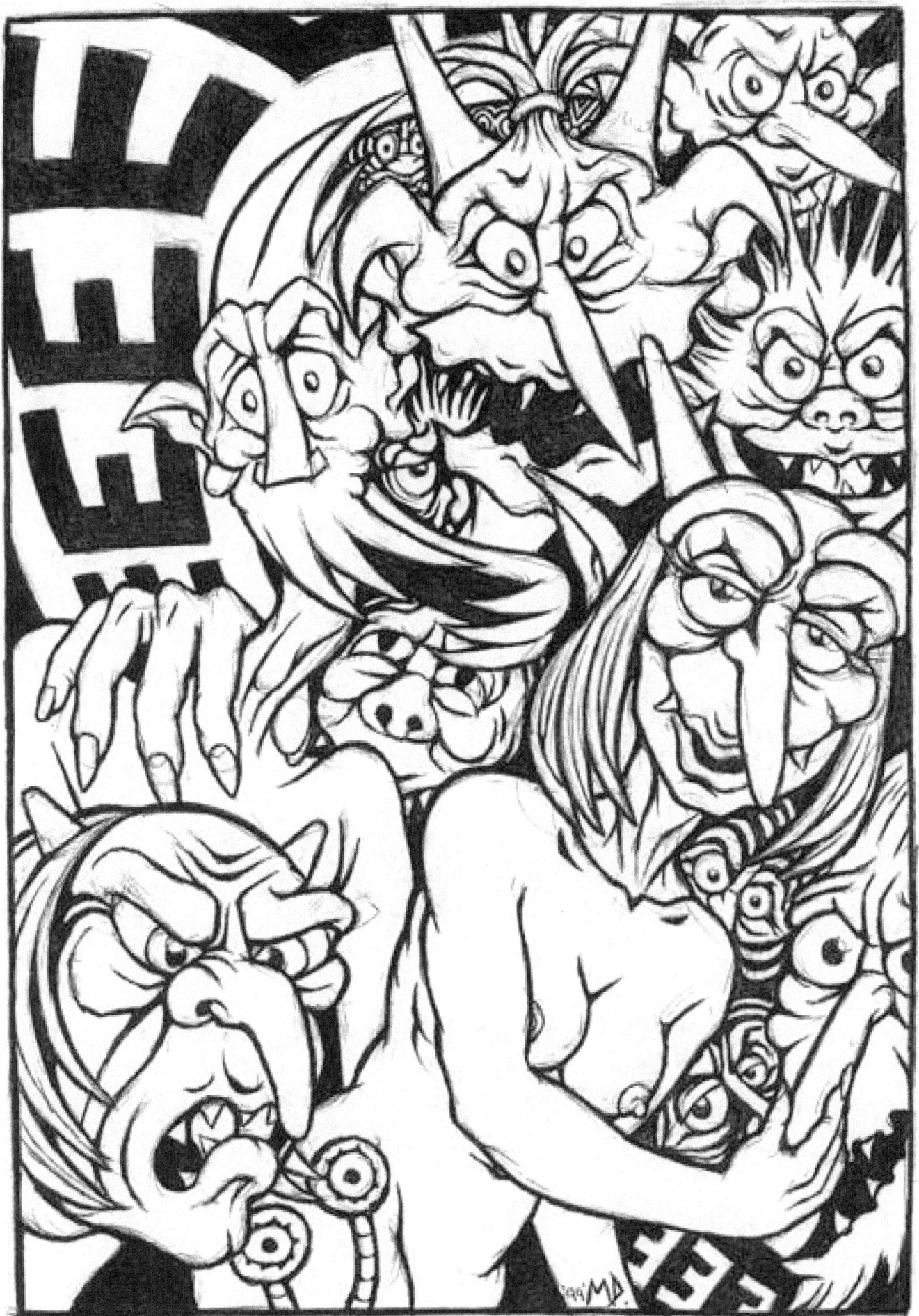

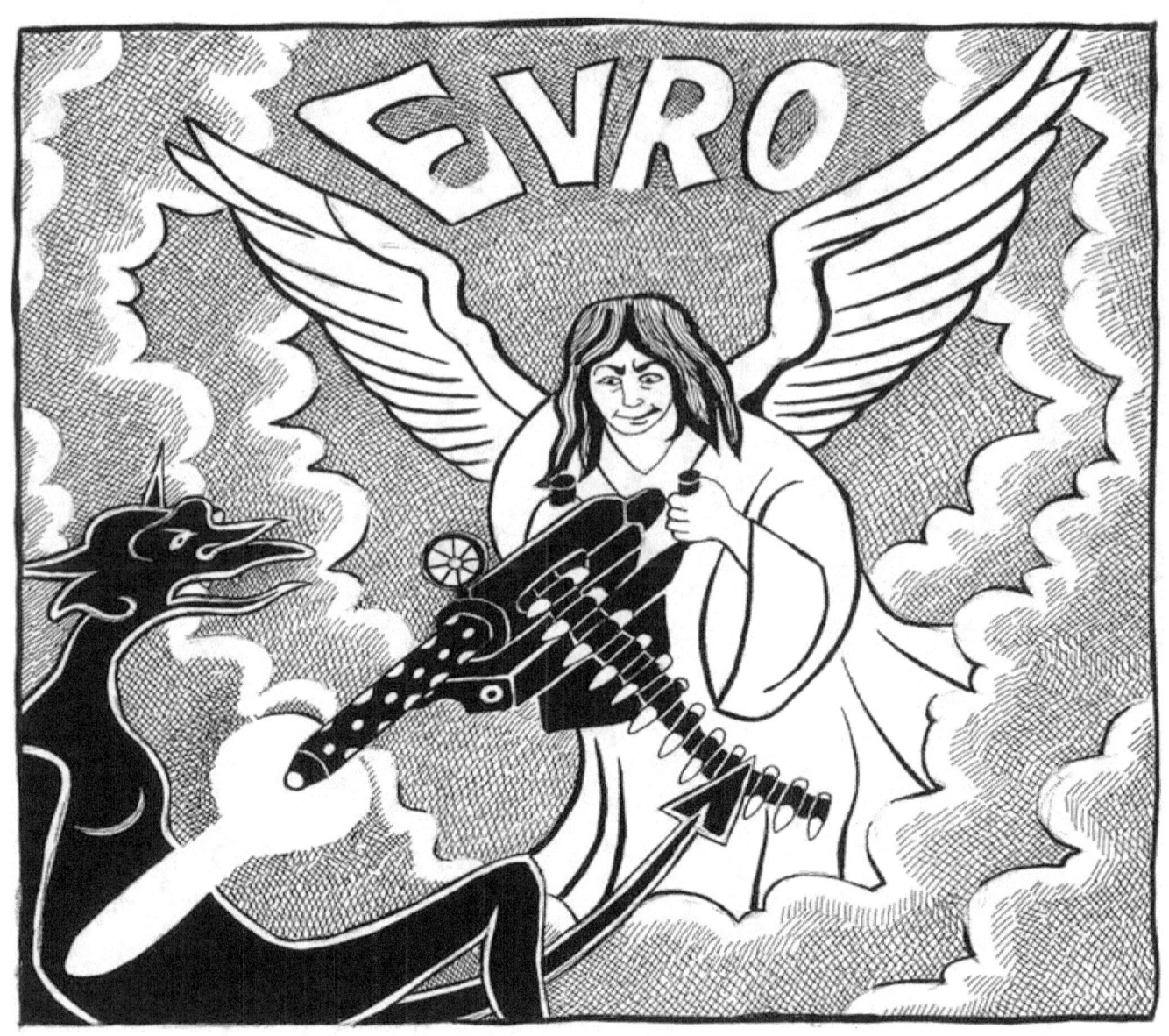

"EVRO"

"EVRO"

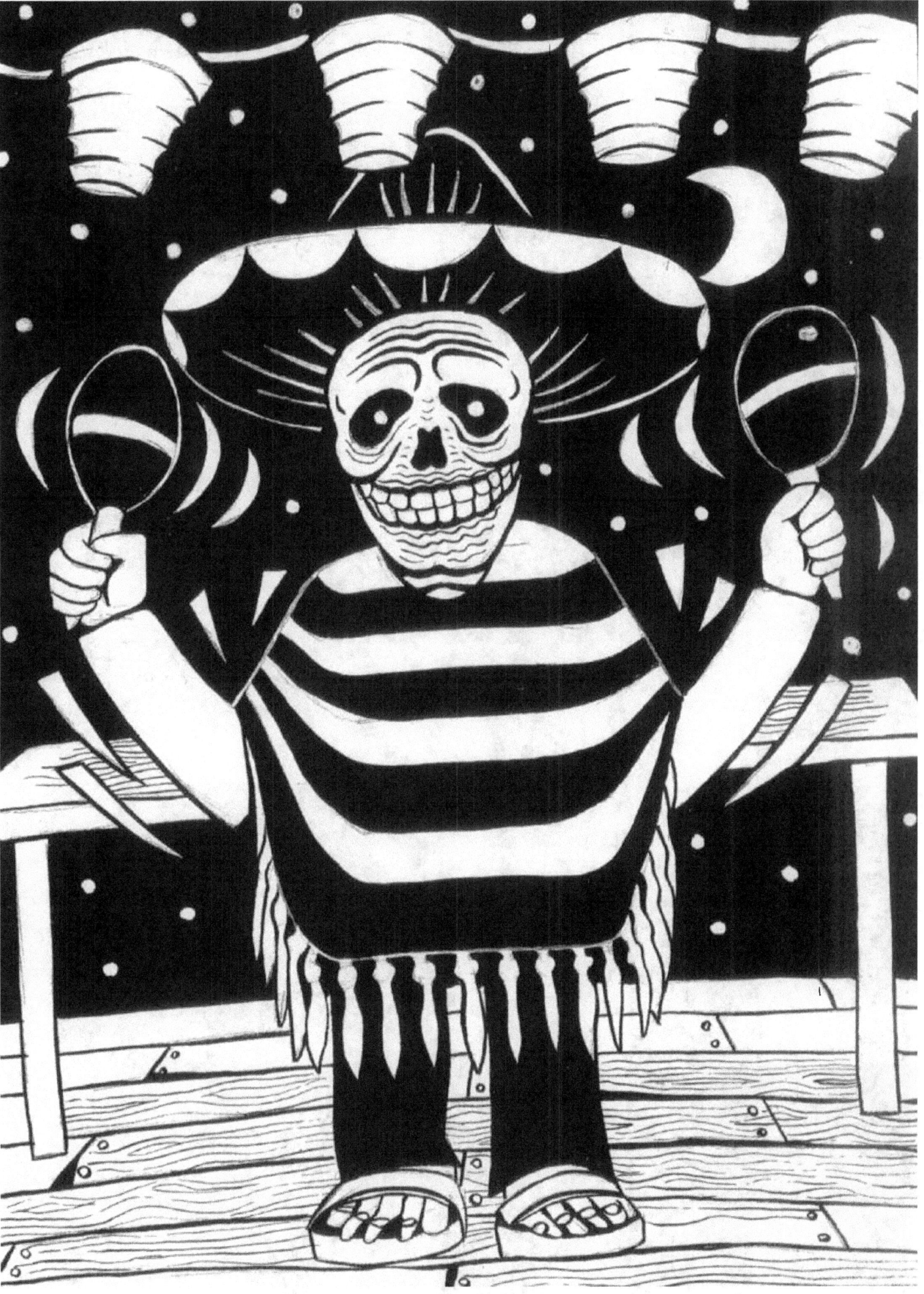

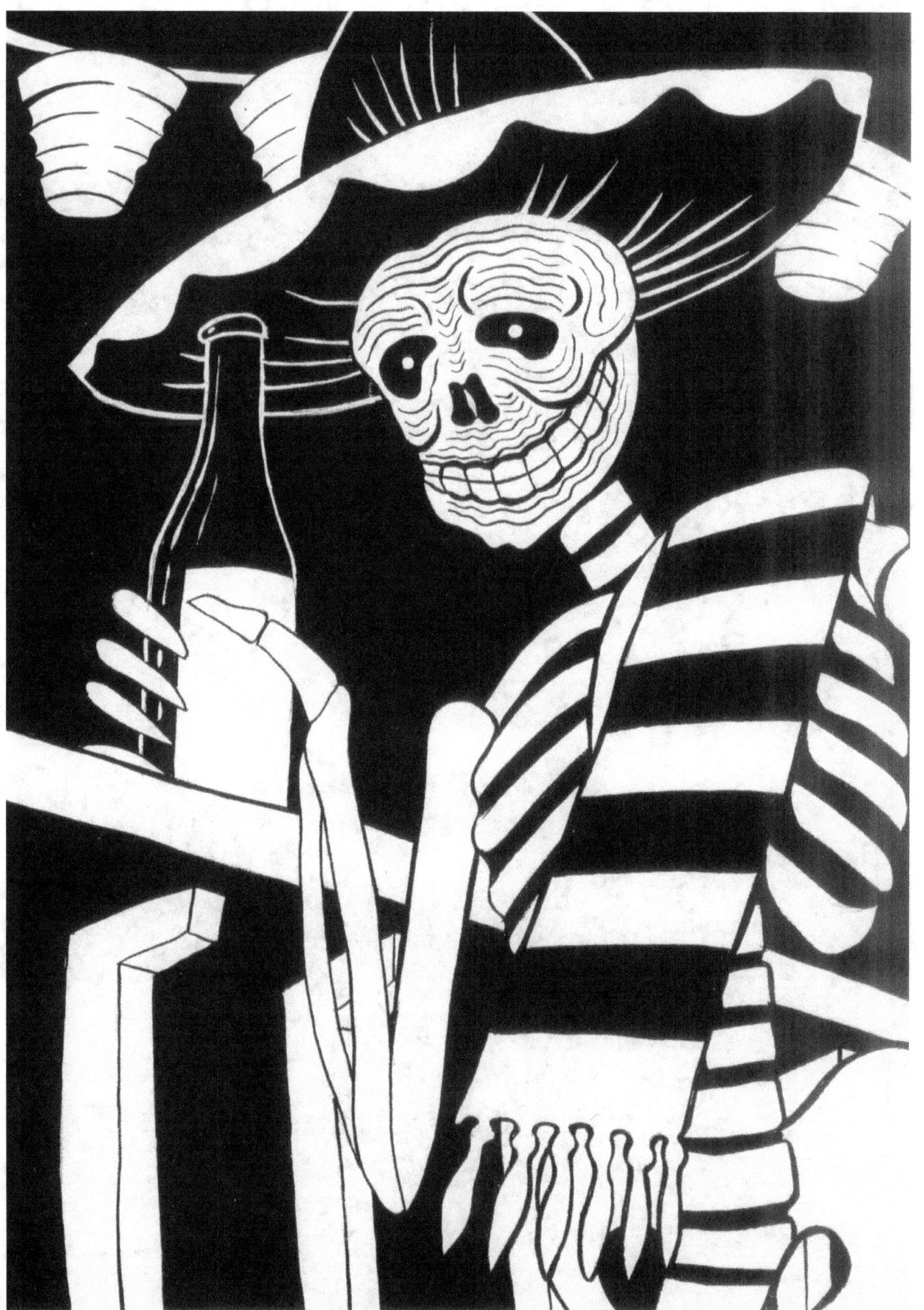

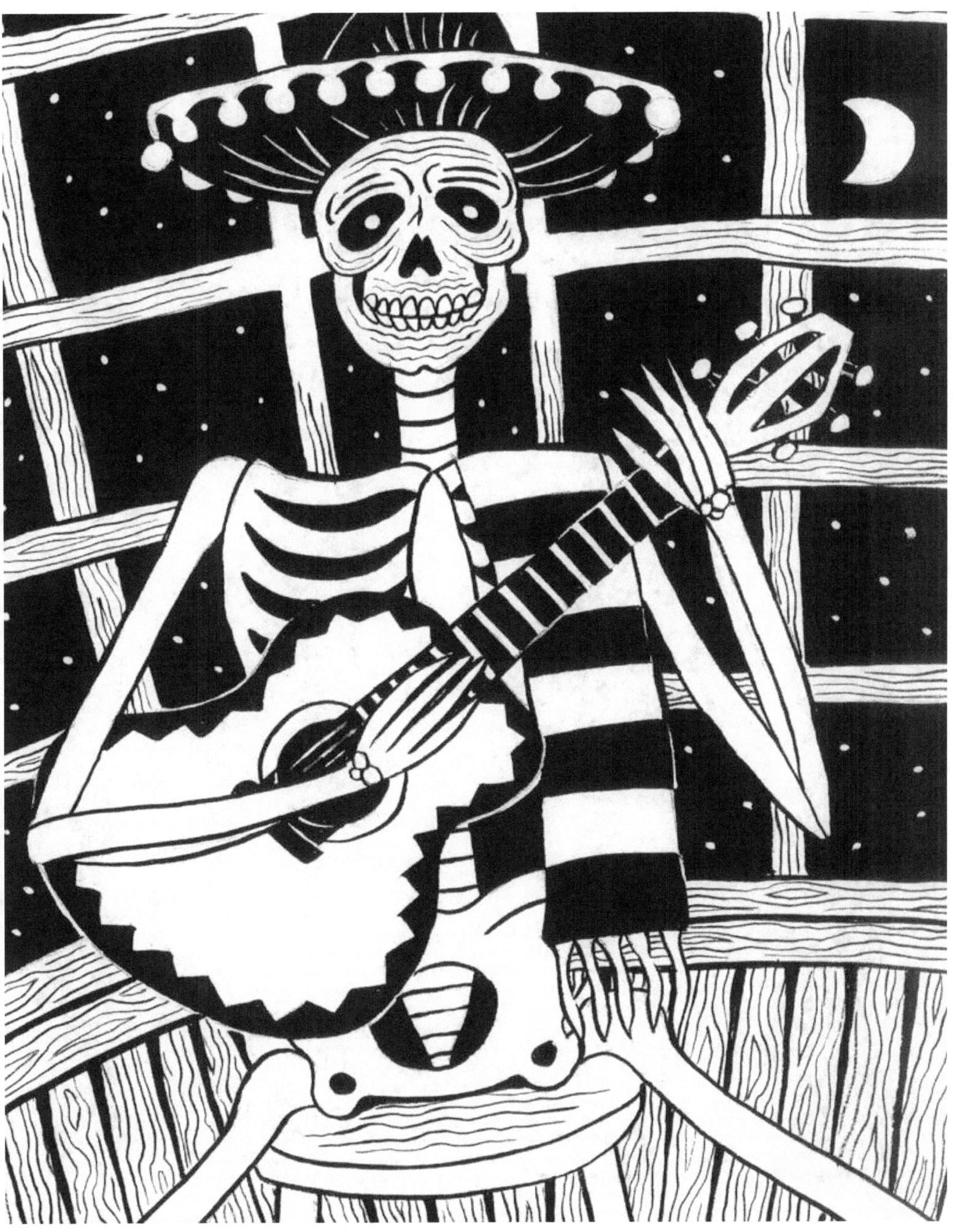

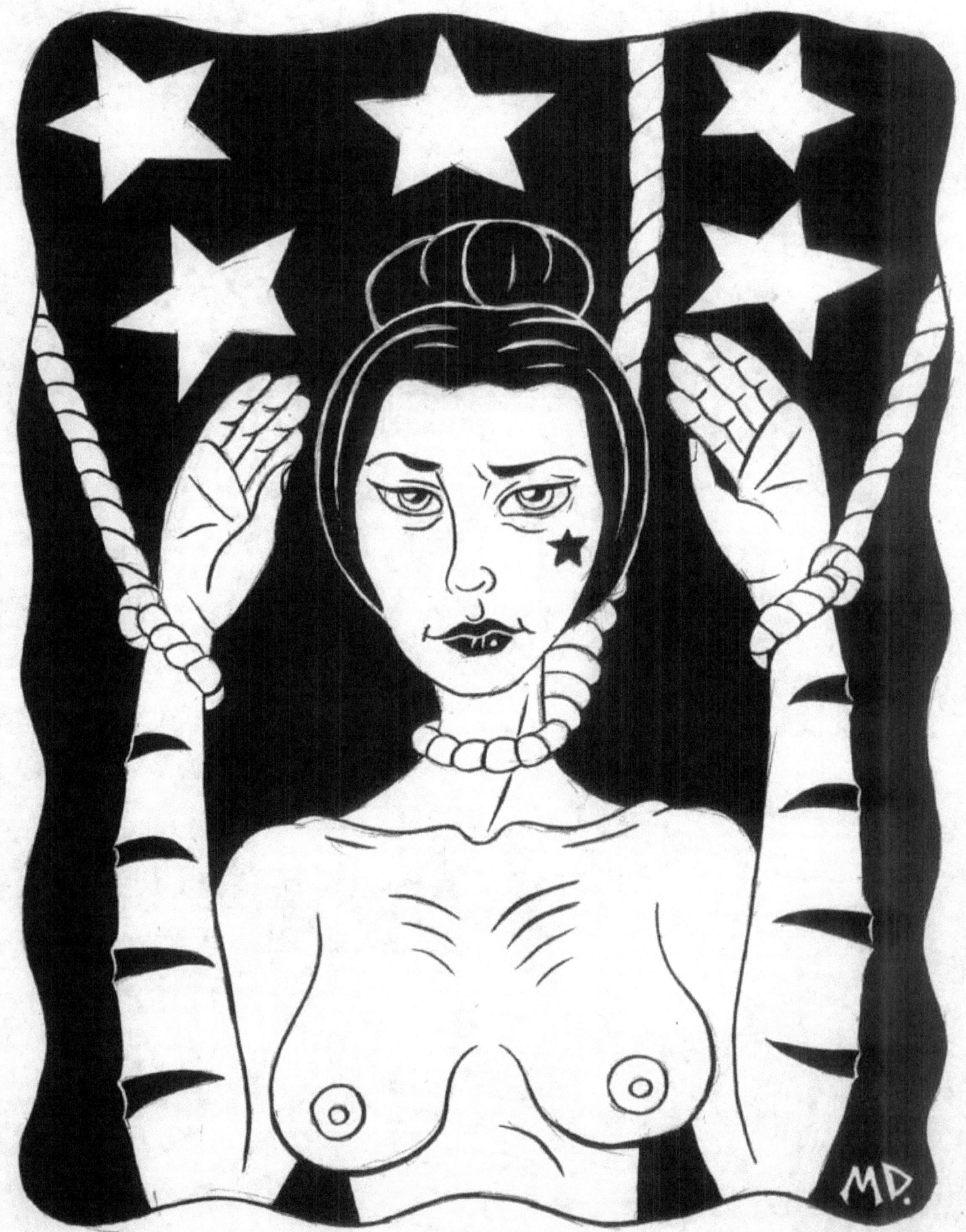

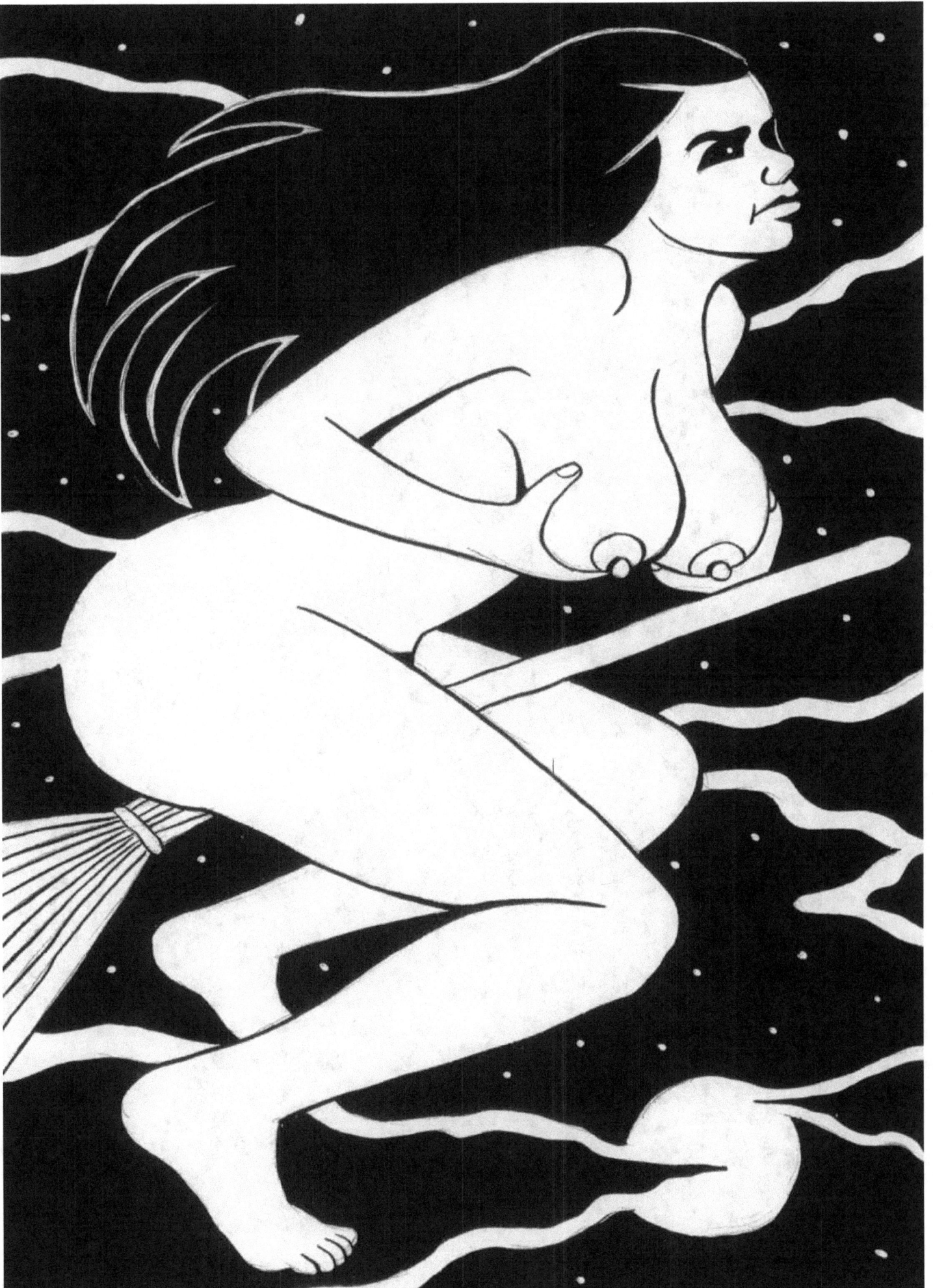

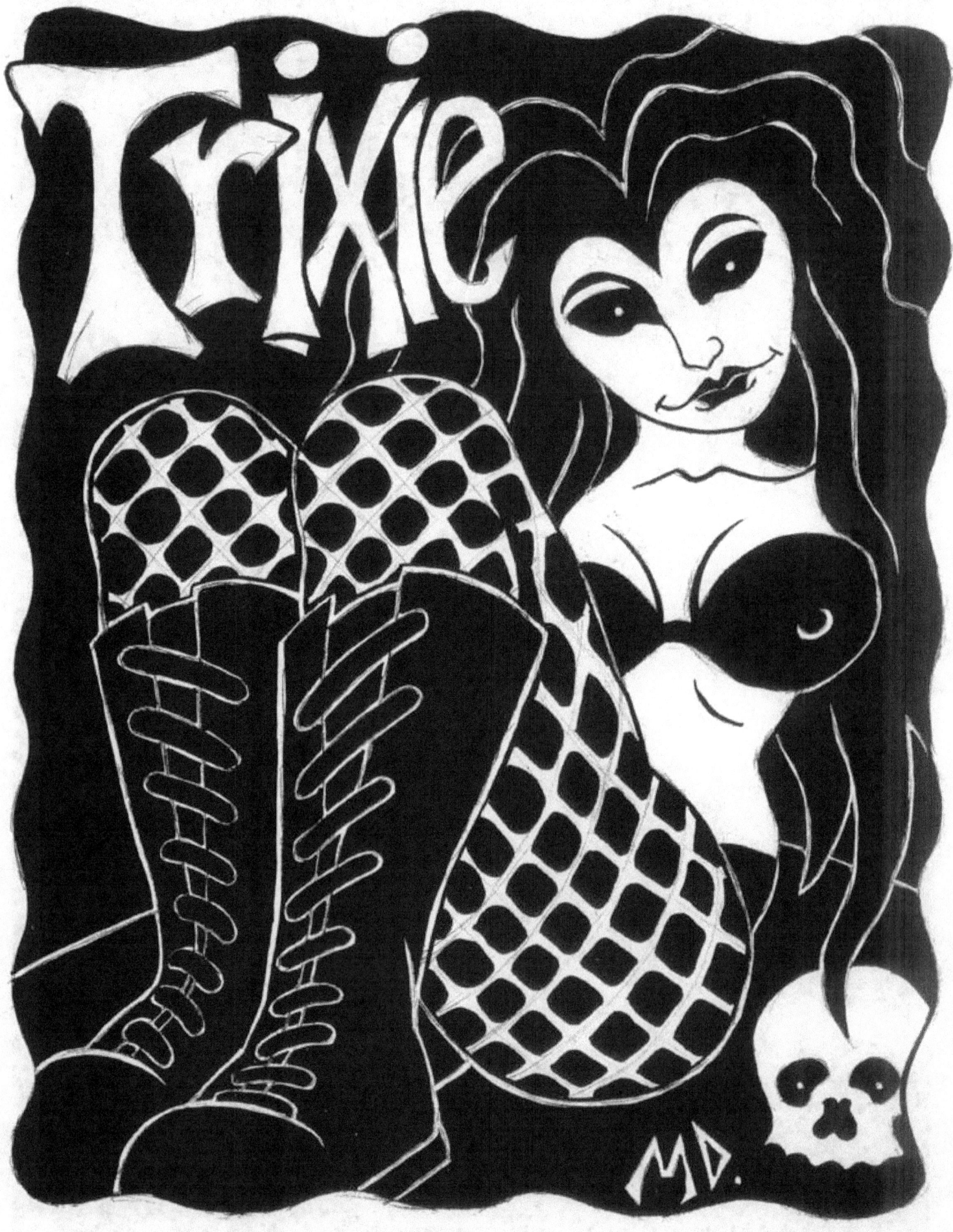

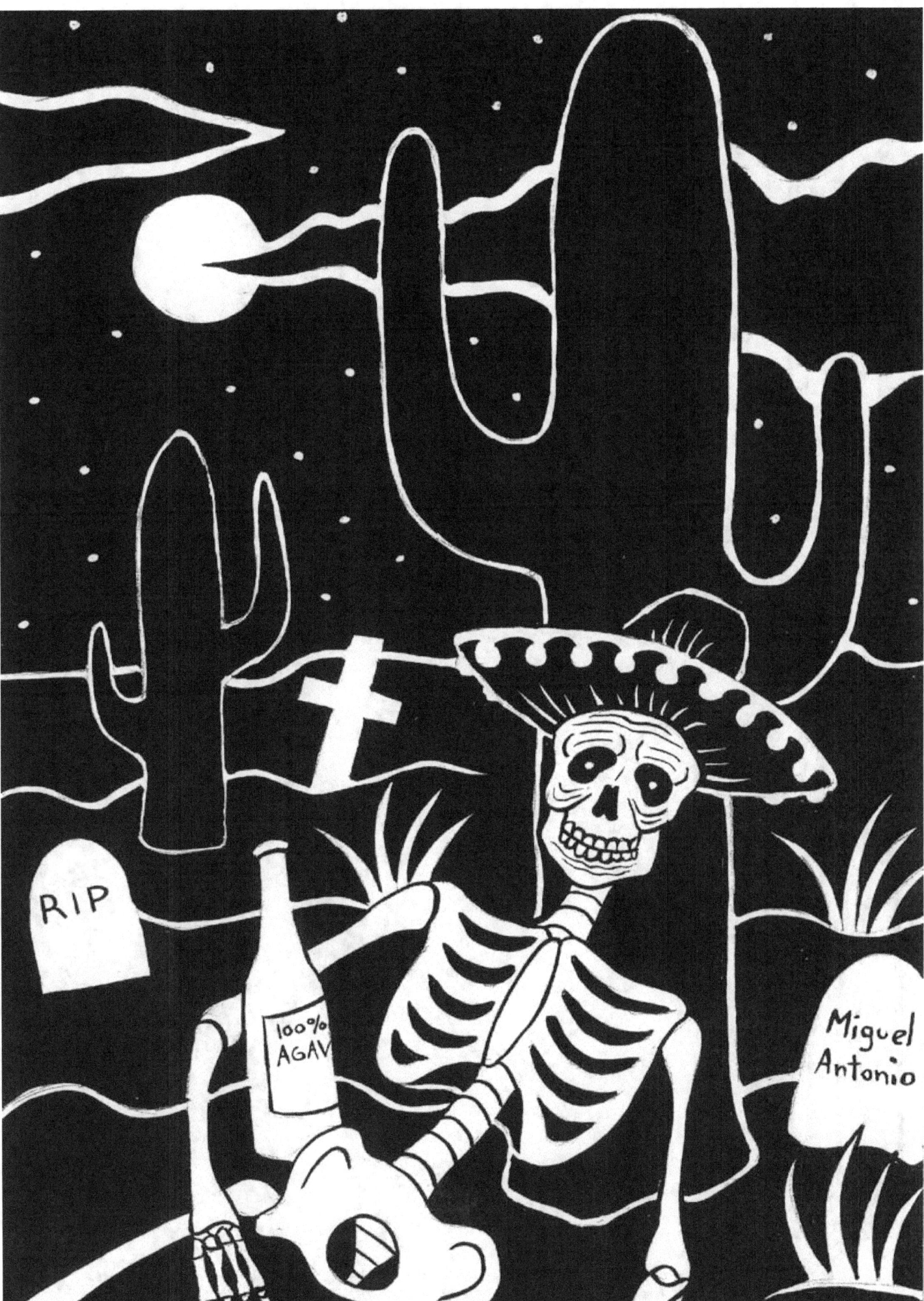

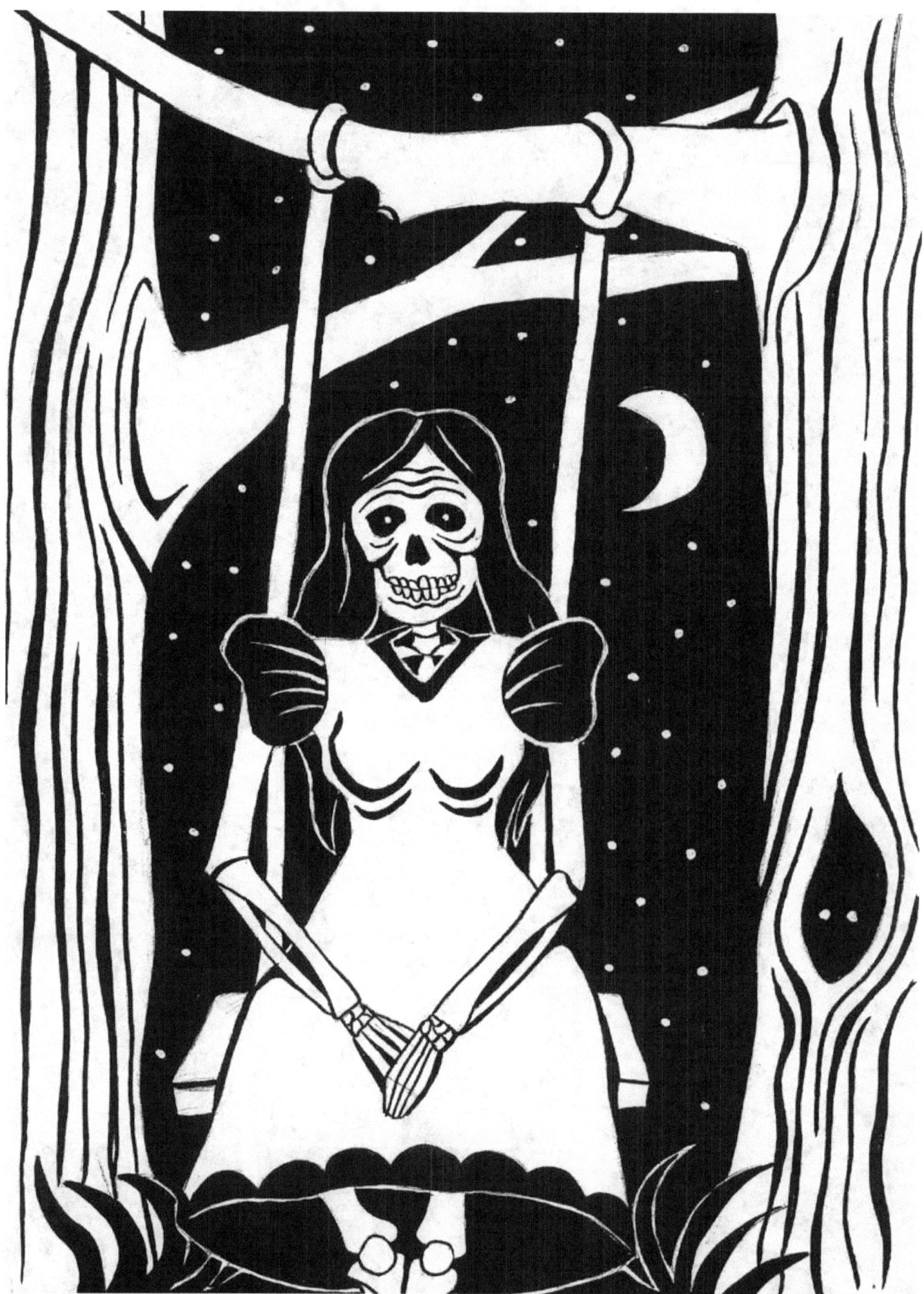

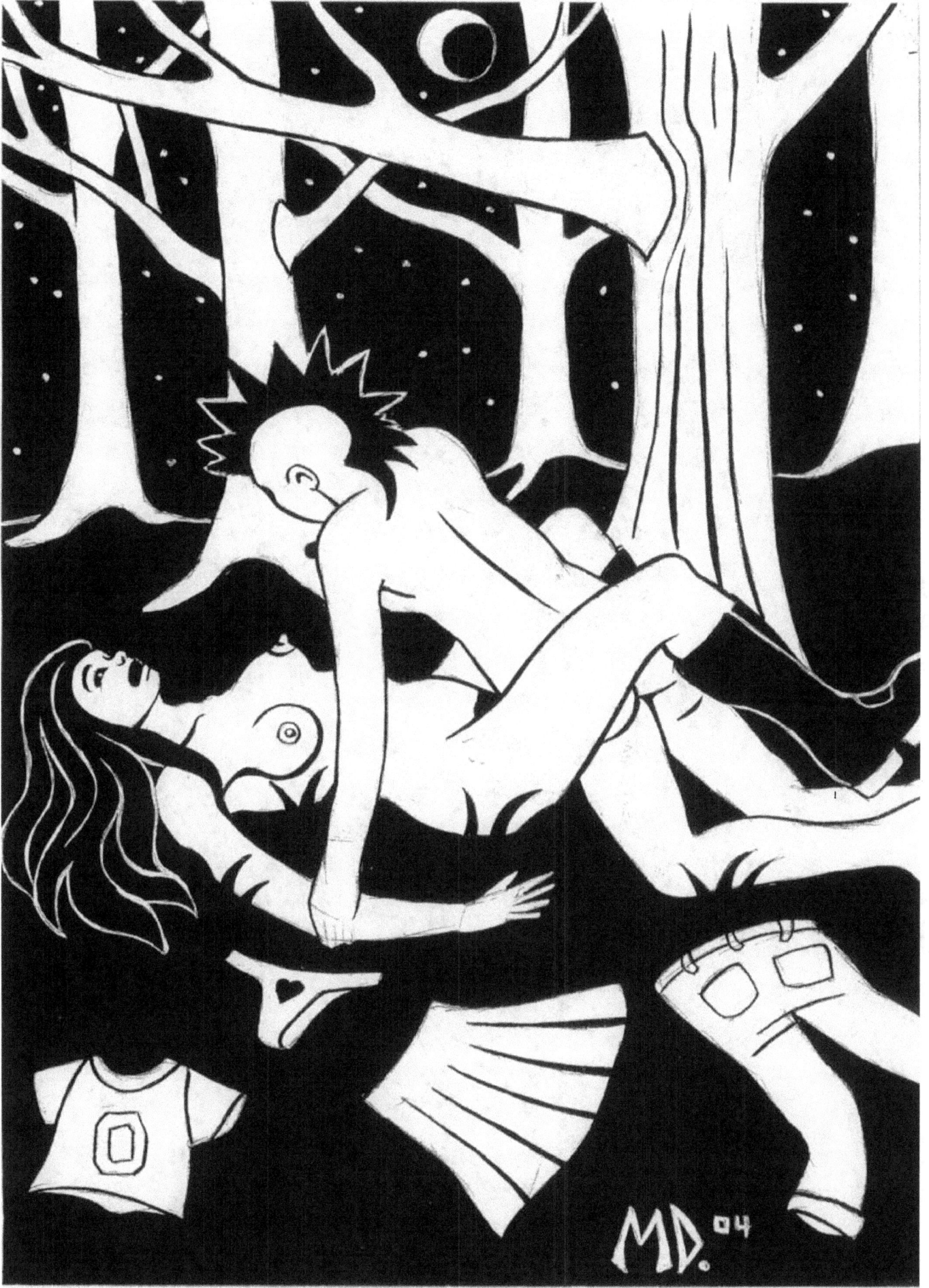

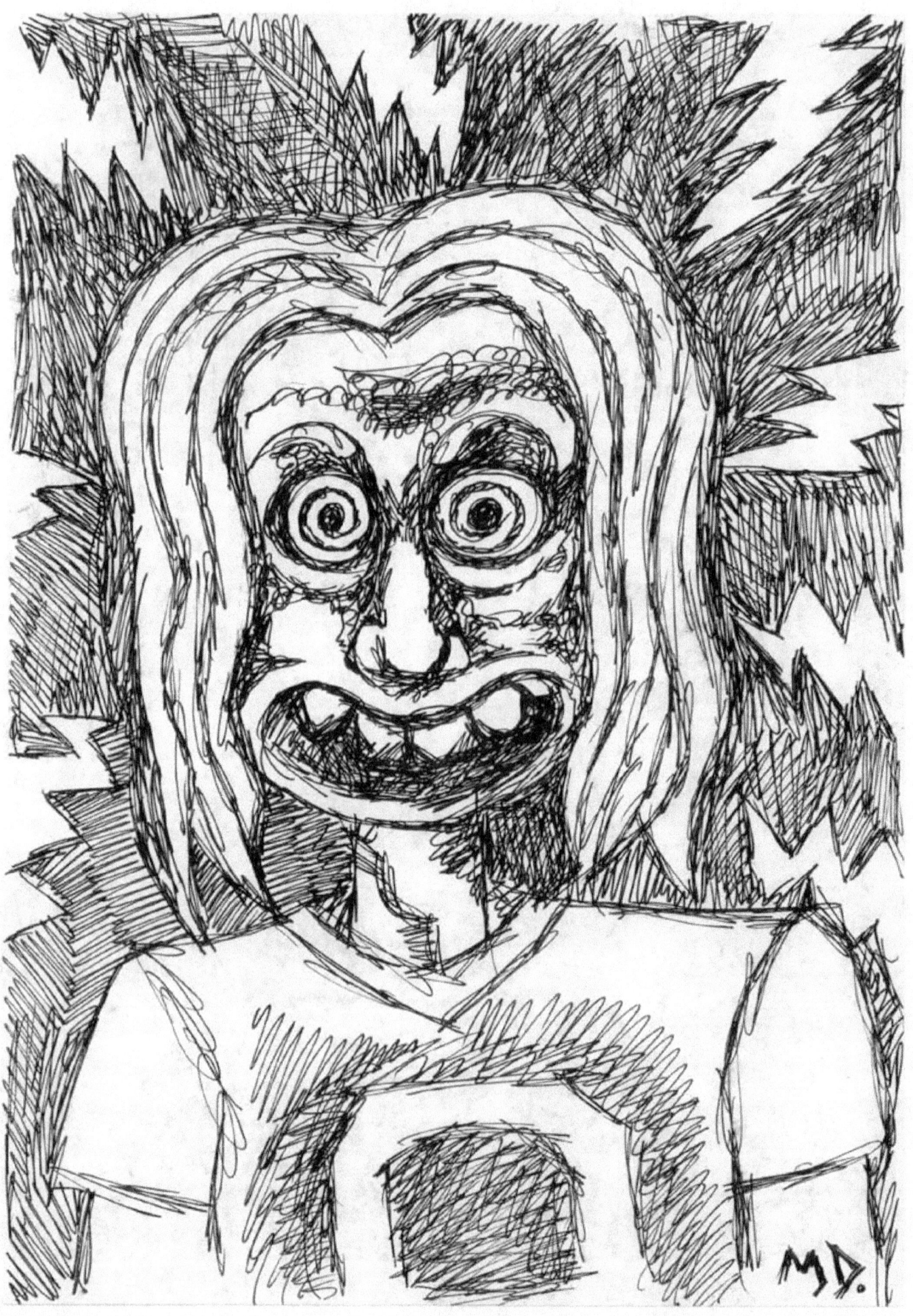

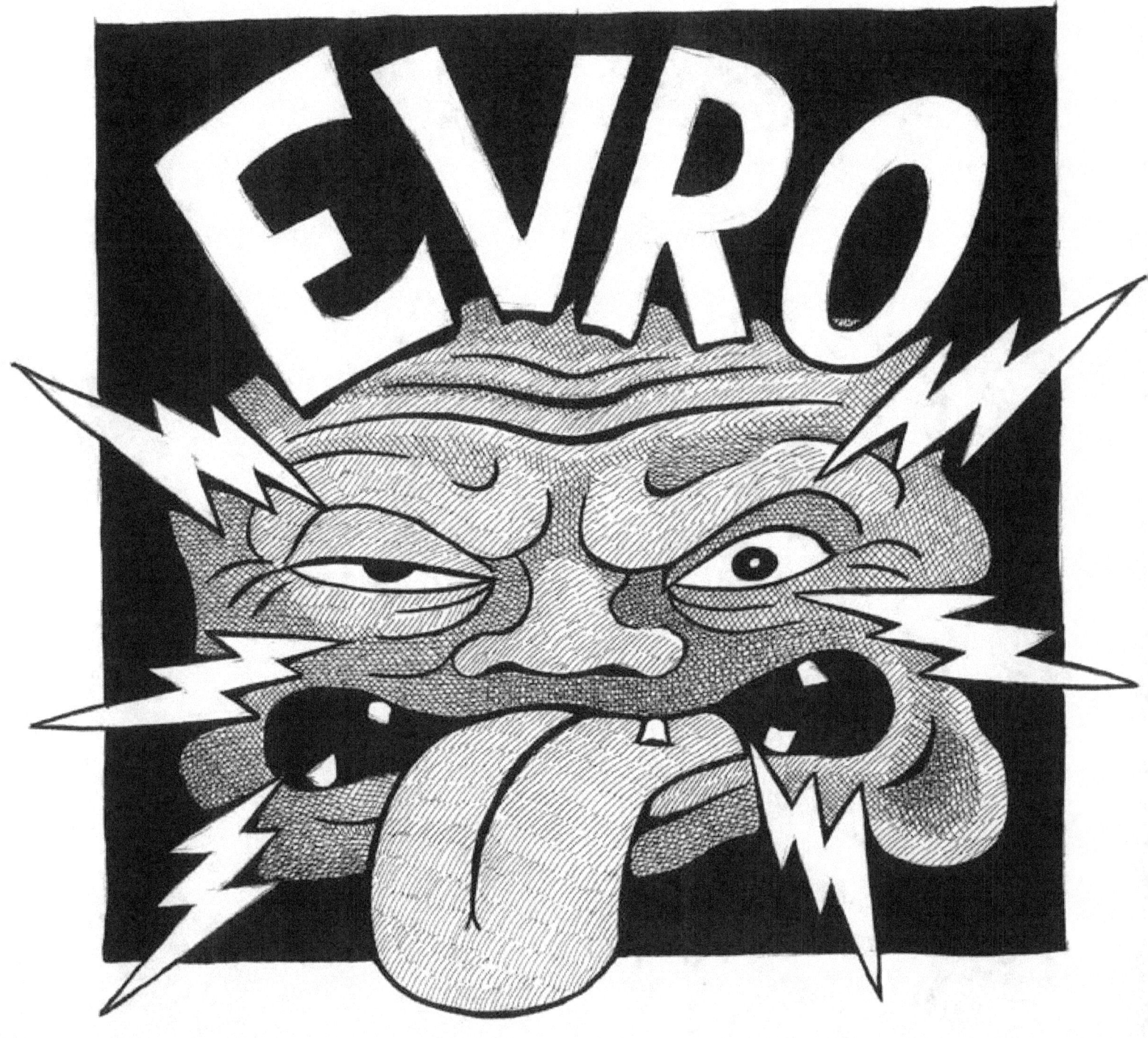

"EVRO #2"

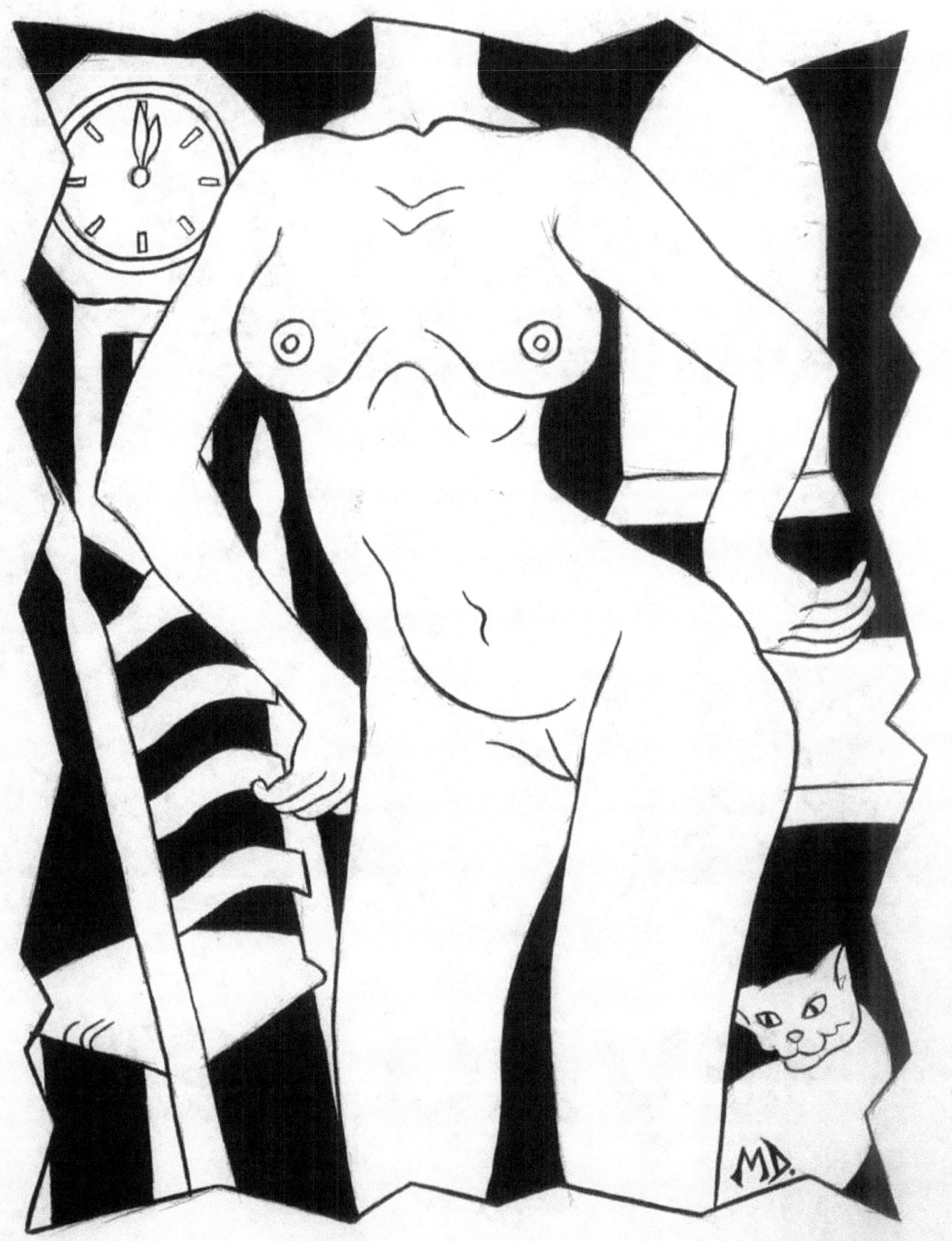

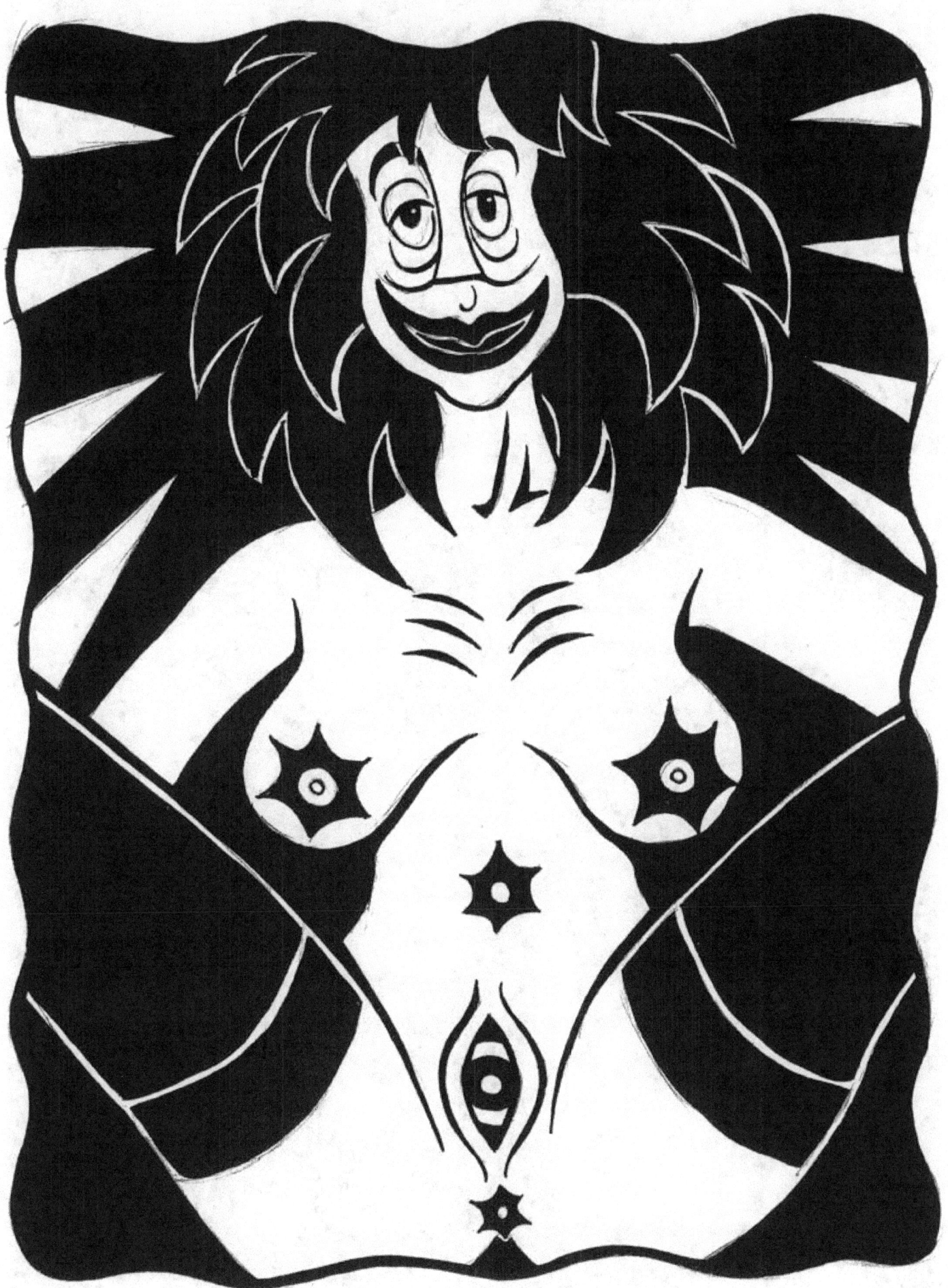

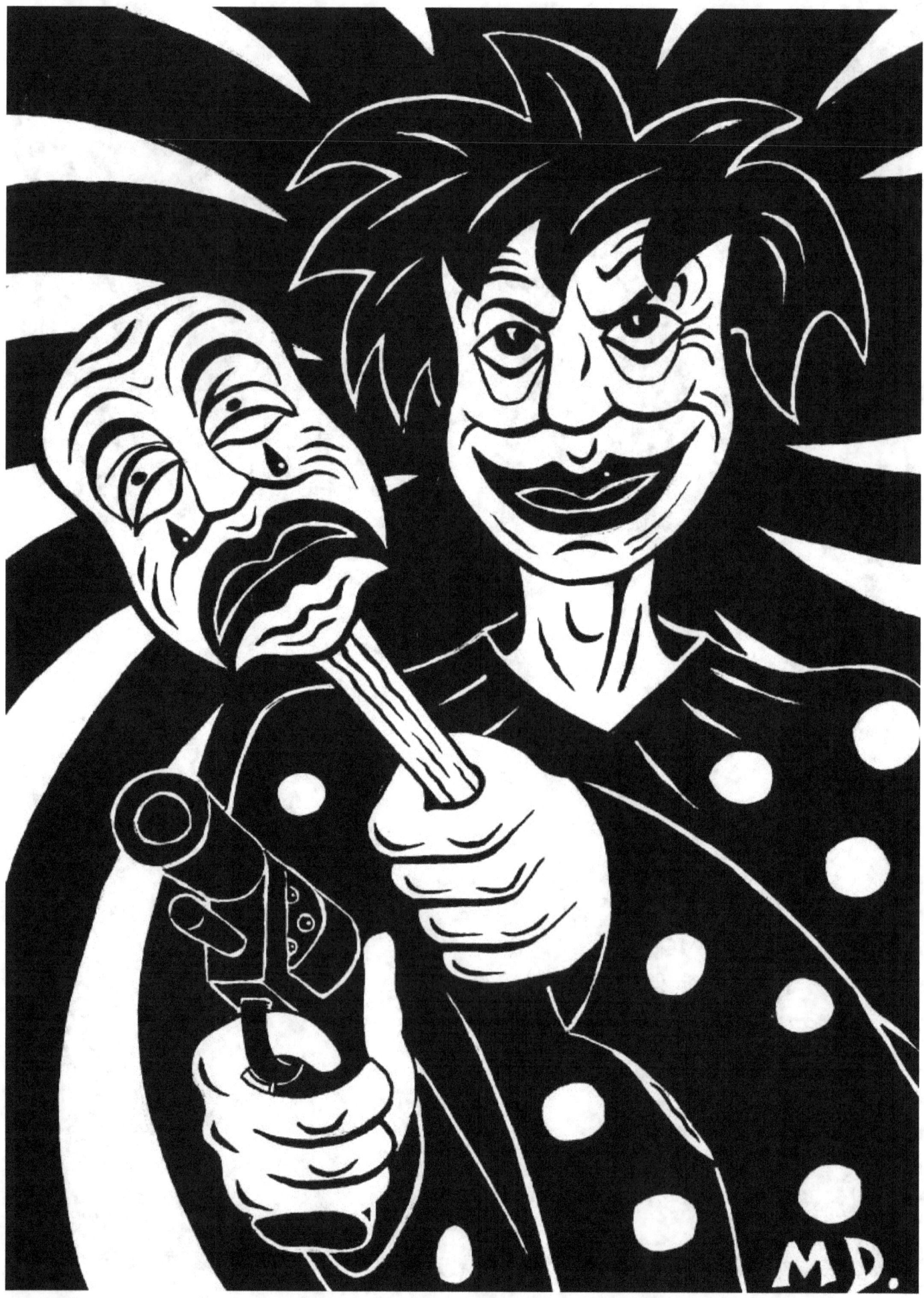

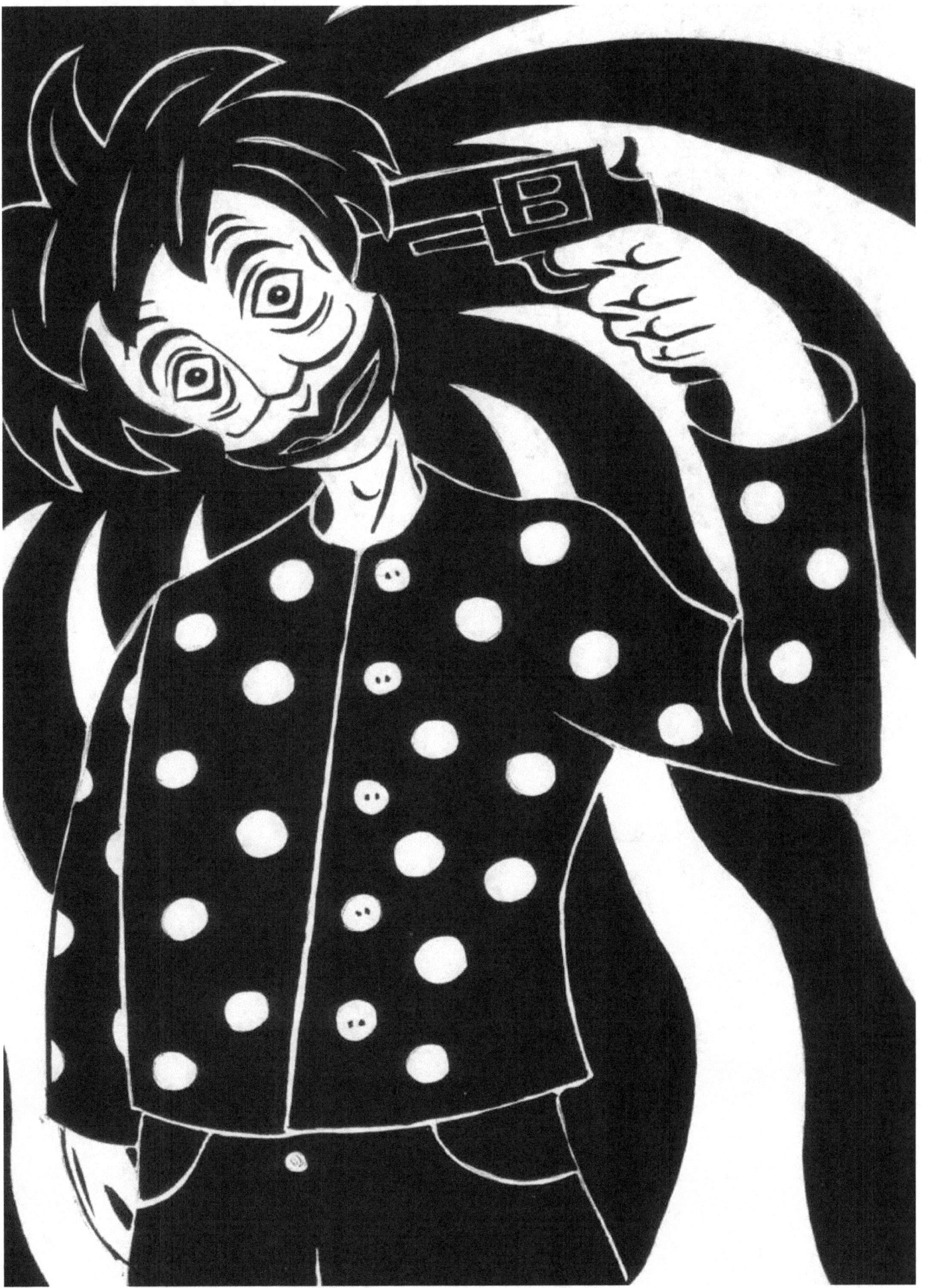

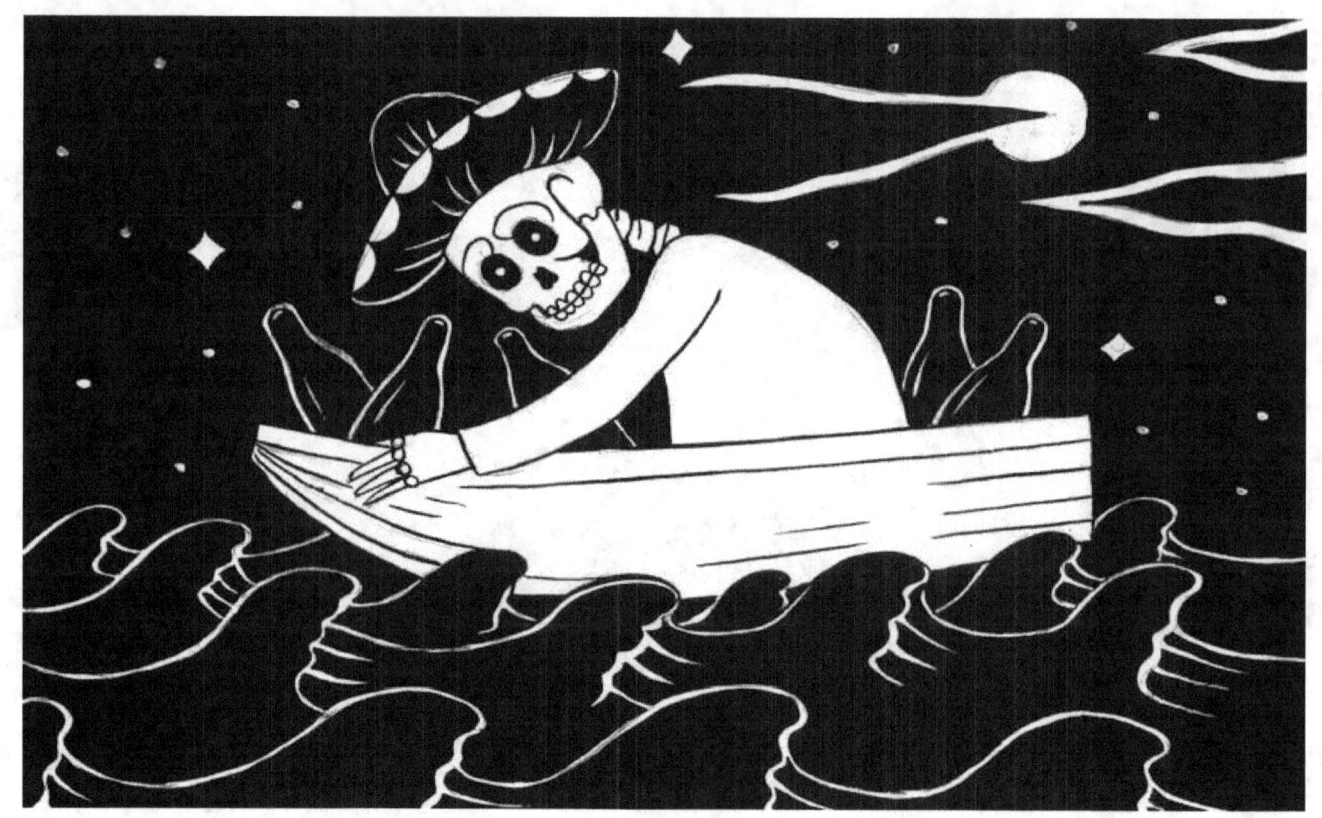

"My little empty boat"

"Alcoholism"

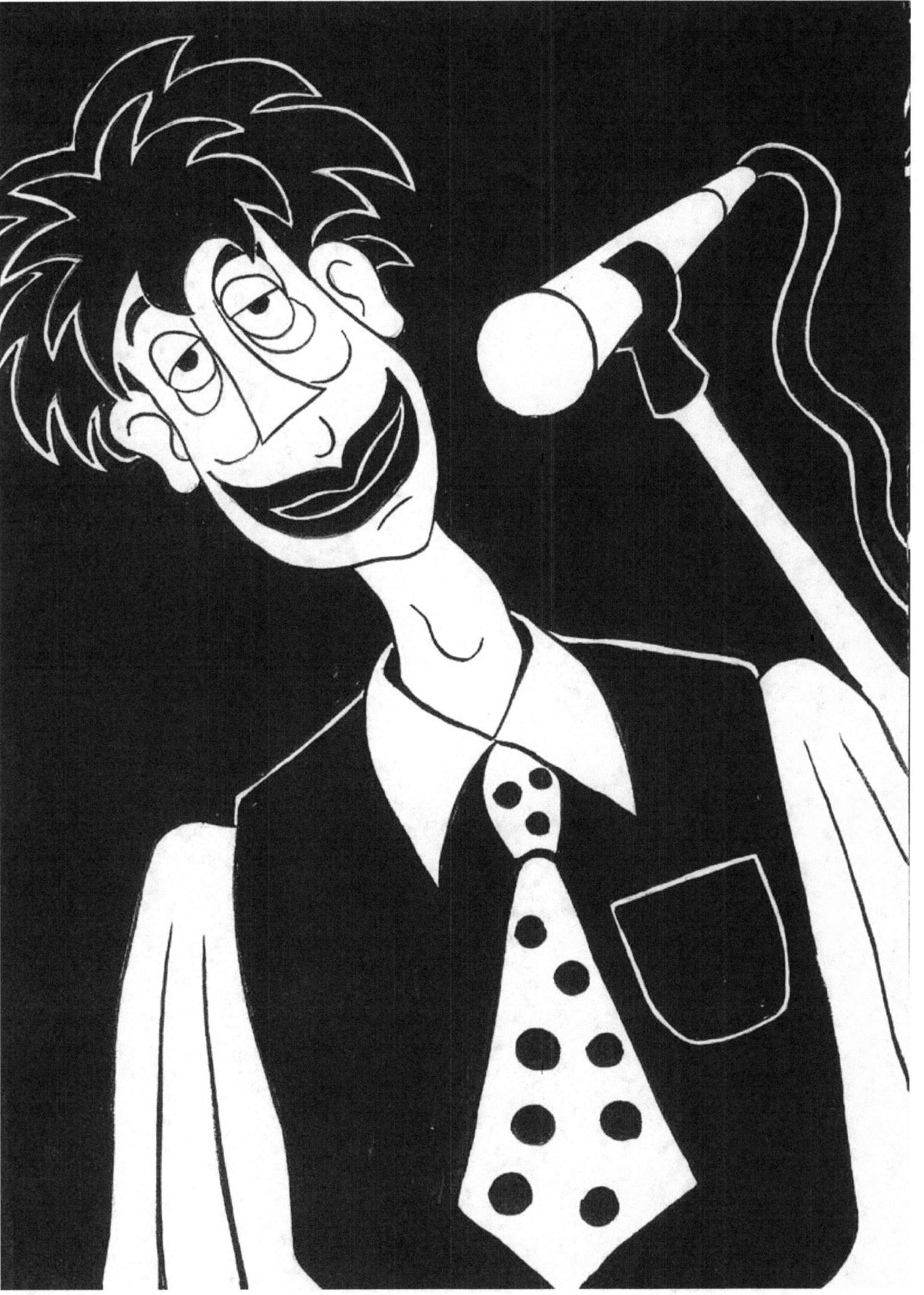

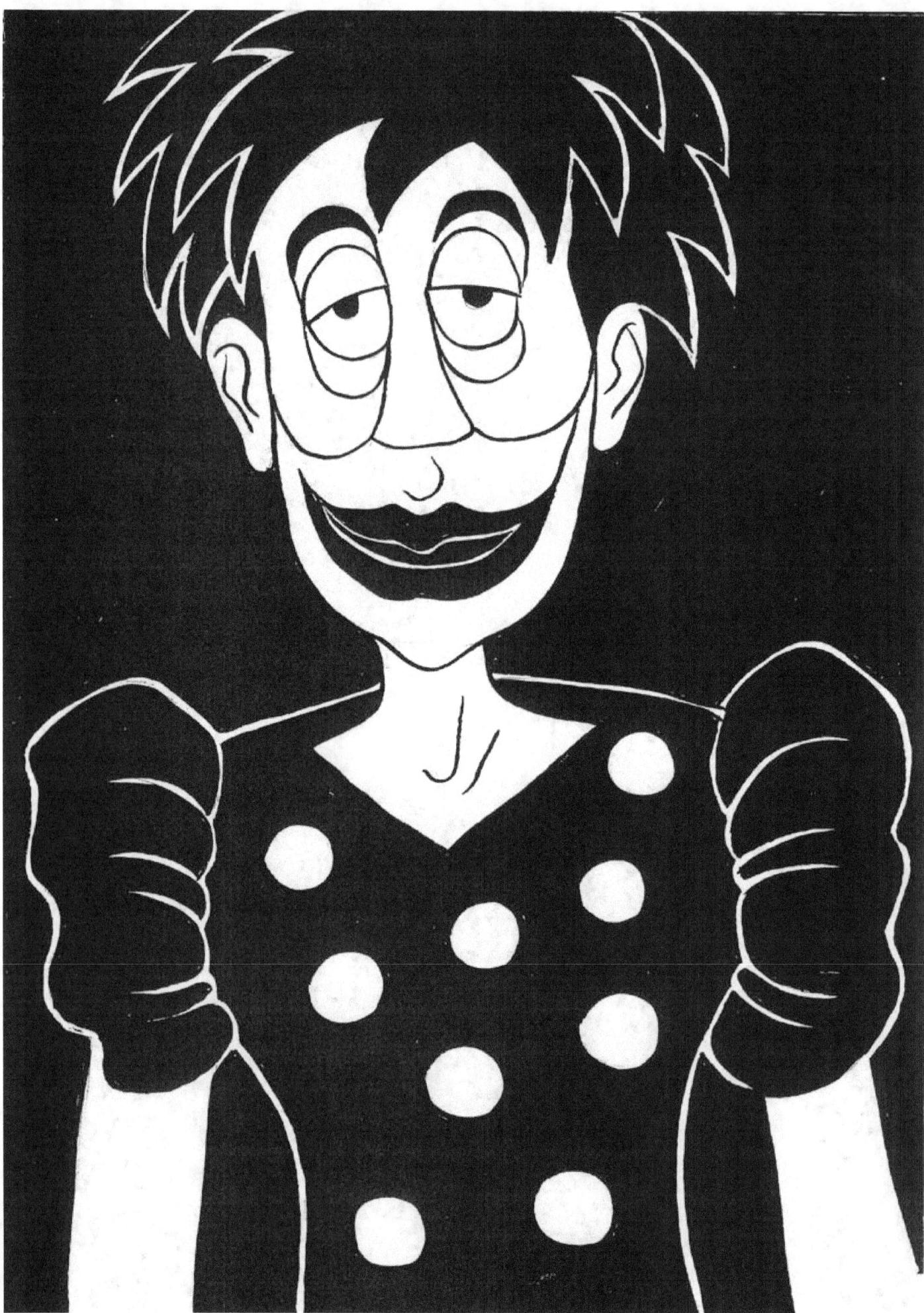

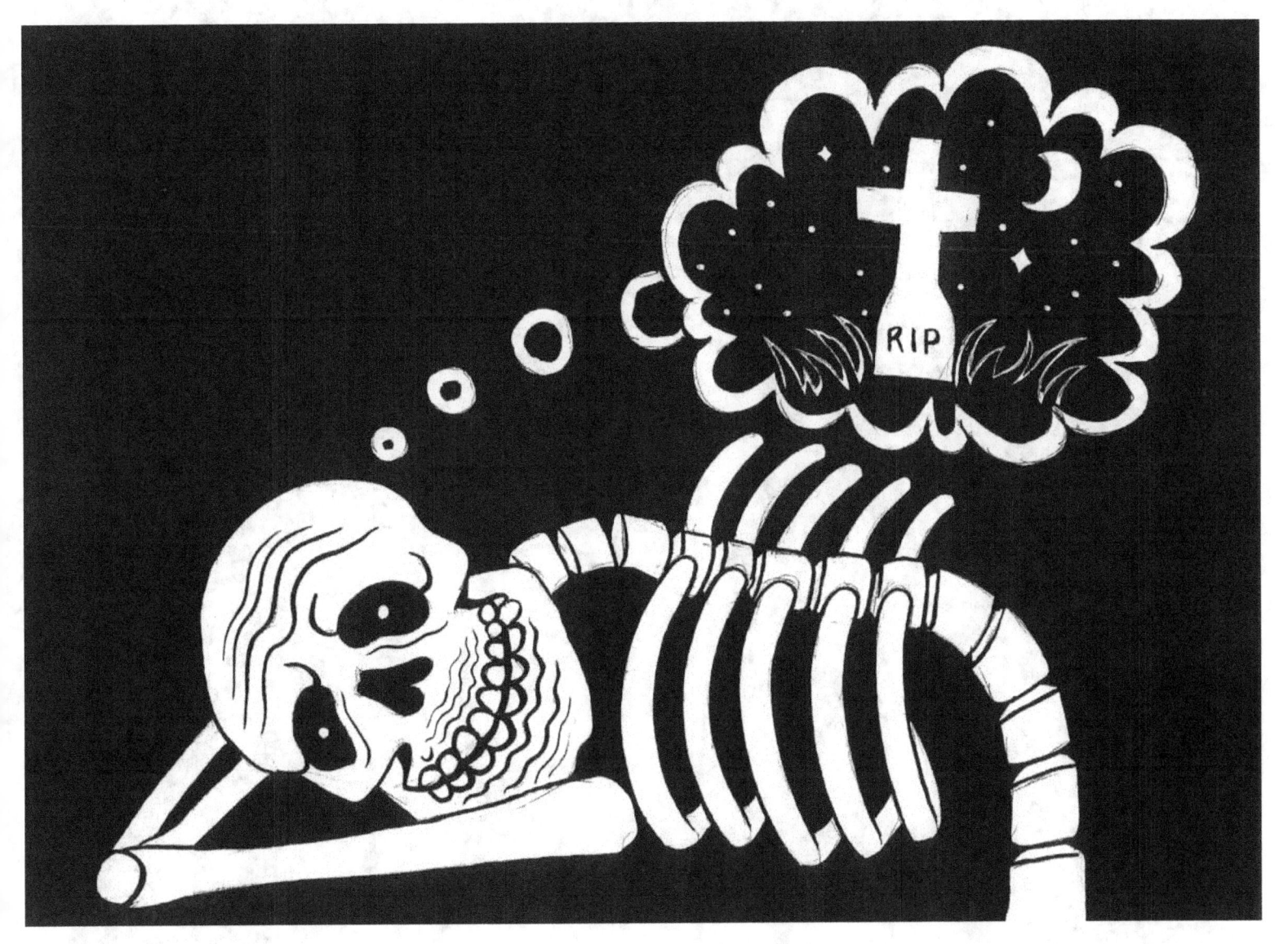

"DEATH DREAM"

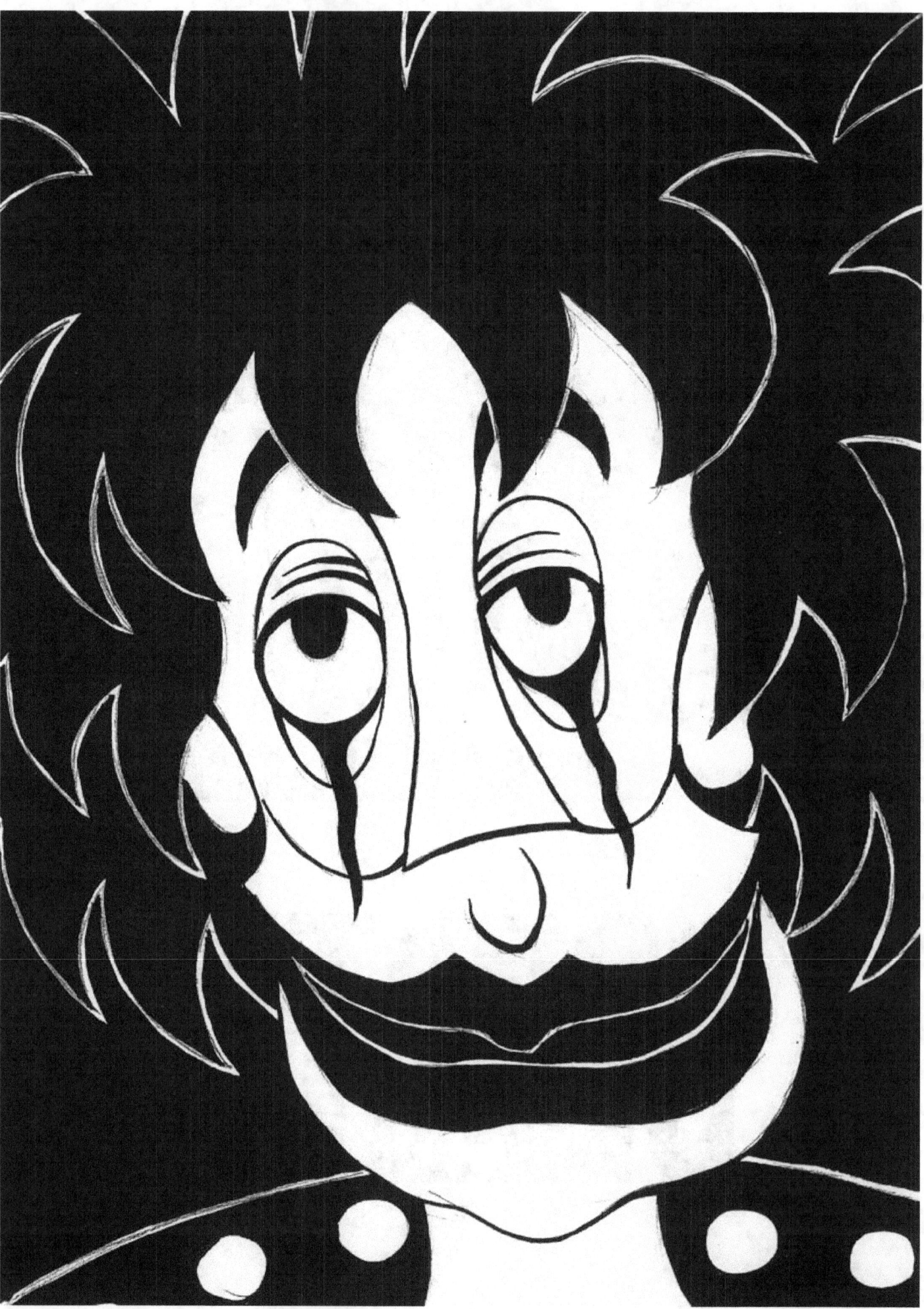

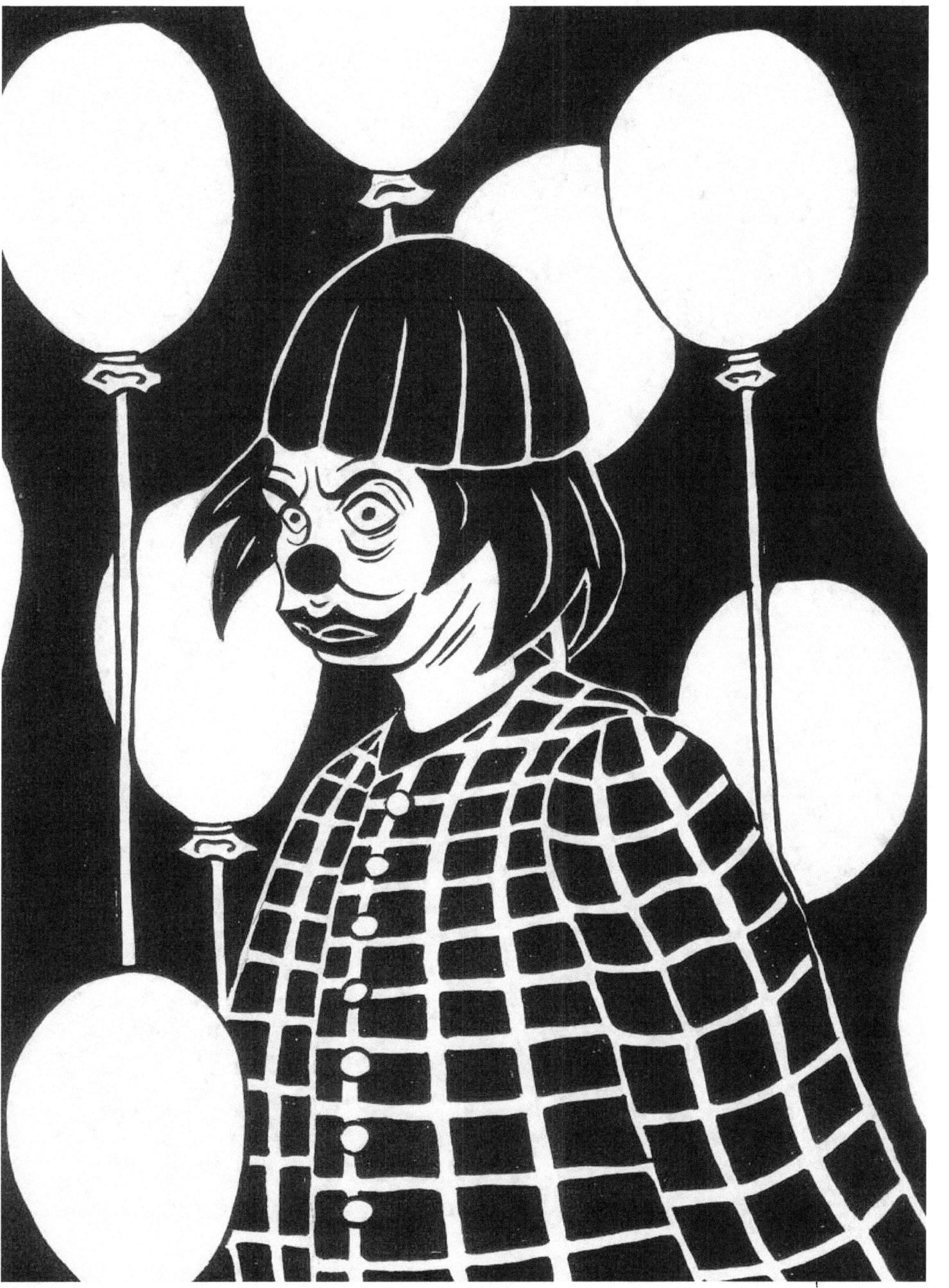

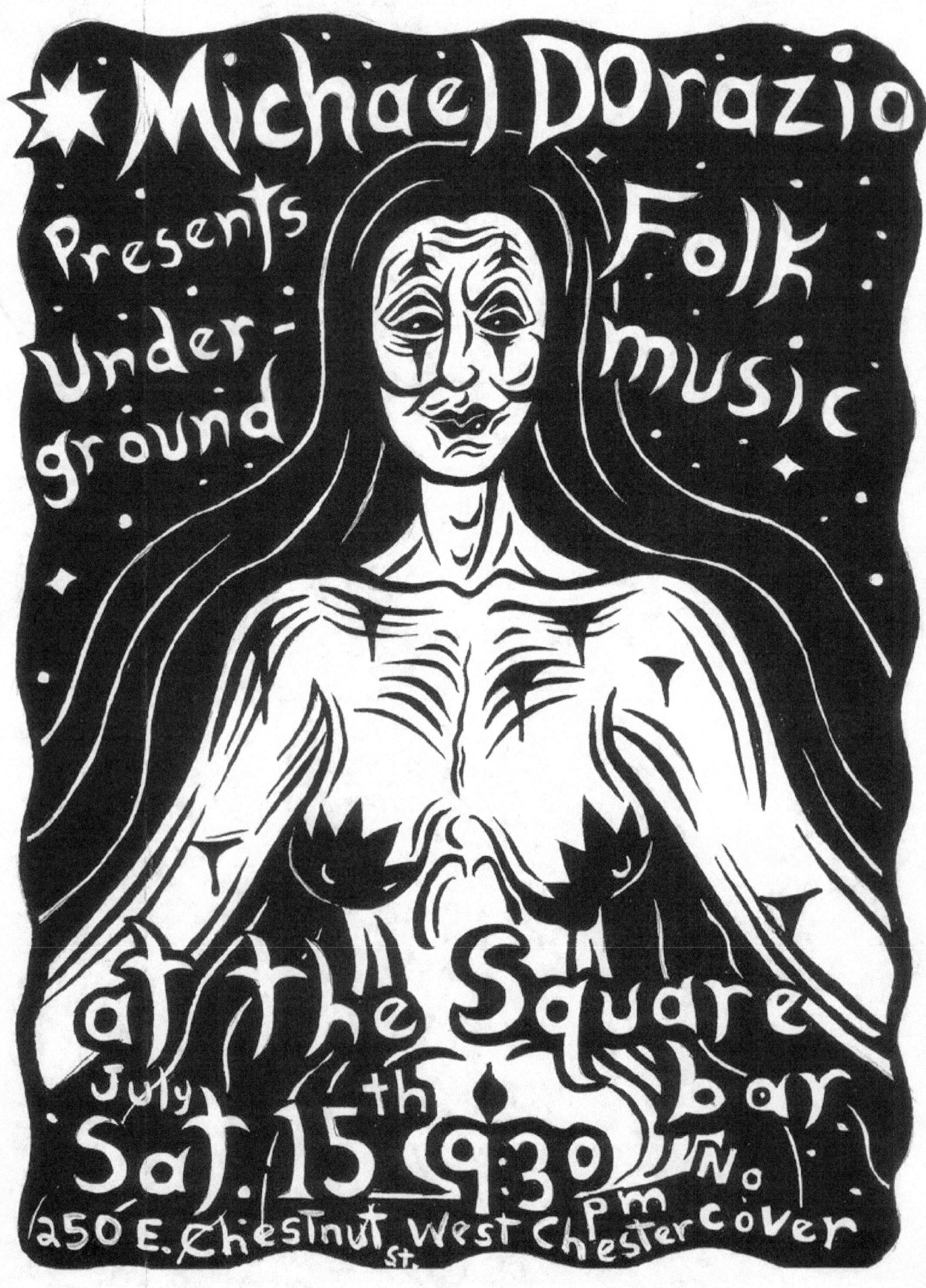

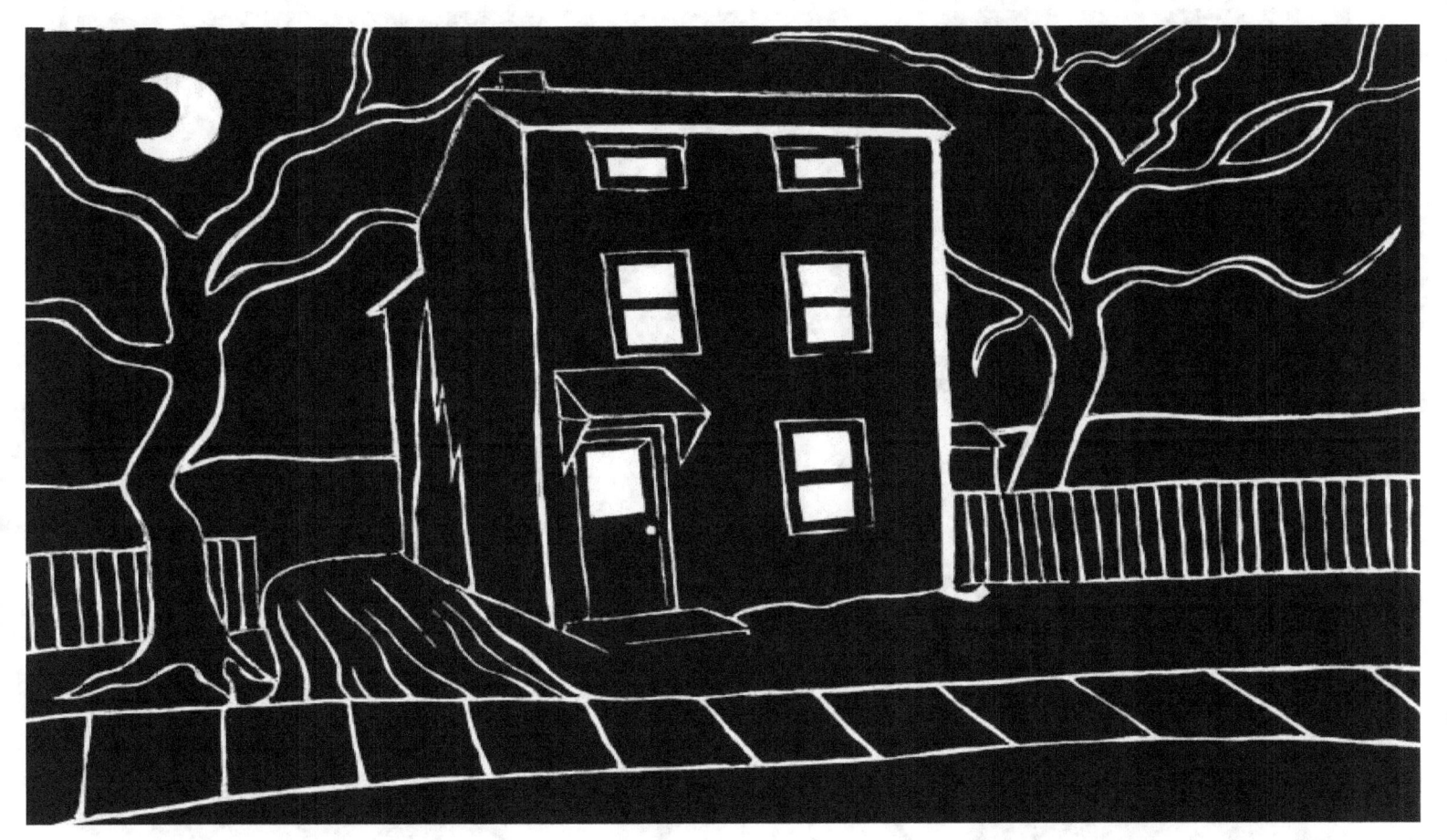

"I came upon a little house, a little house upon the hill. " "Into the house with it's blood red bowels, with wet lipped women with greasy fists crawled on the ceilings and walls" ---Nick Cave

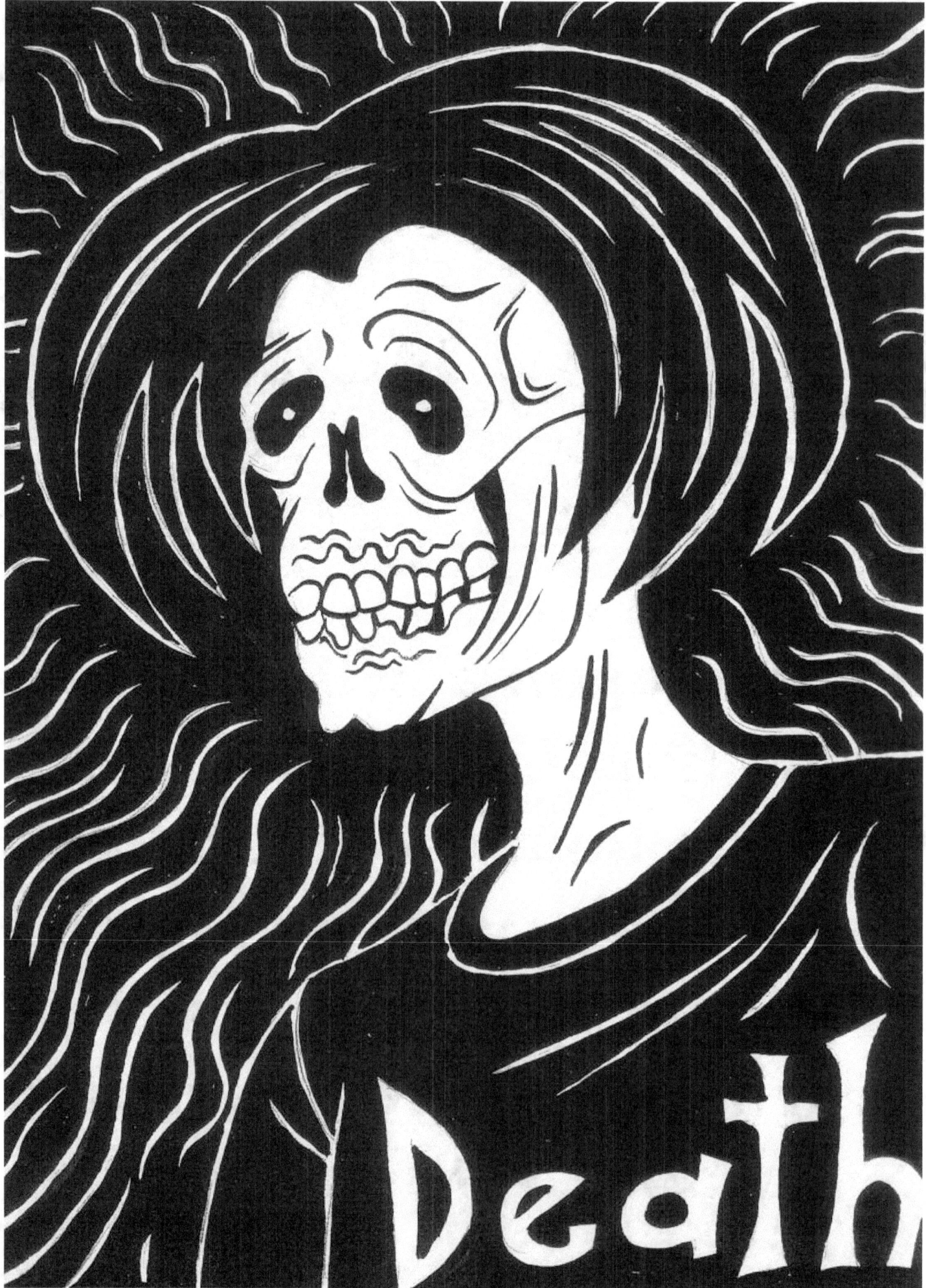

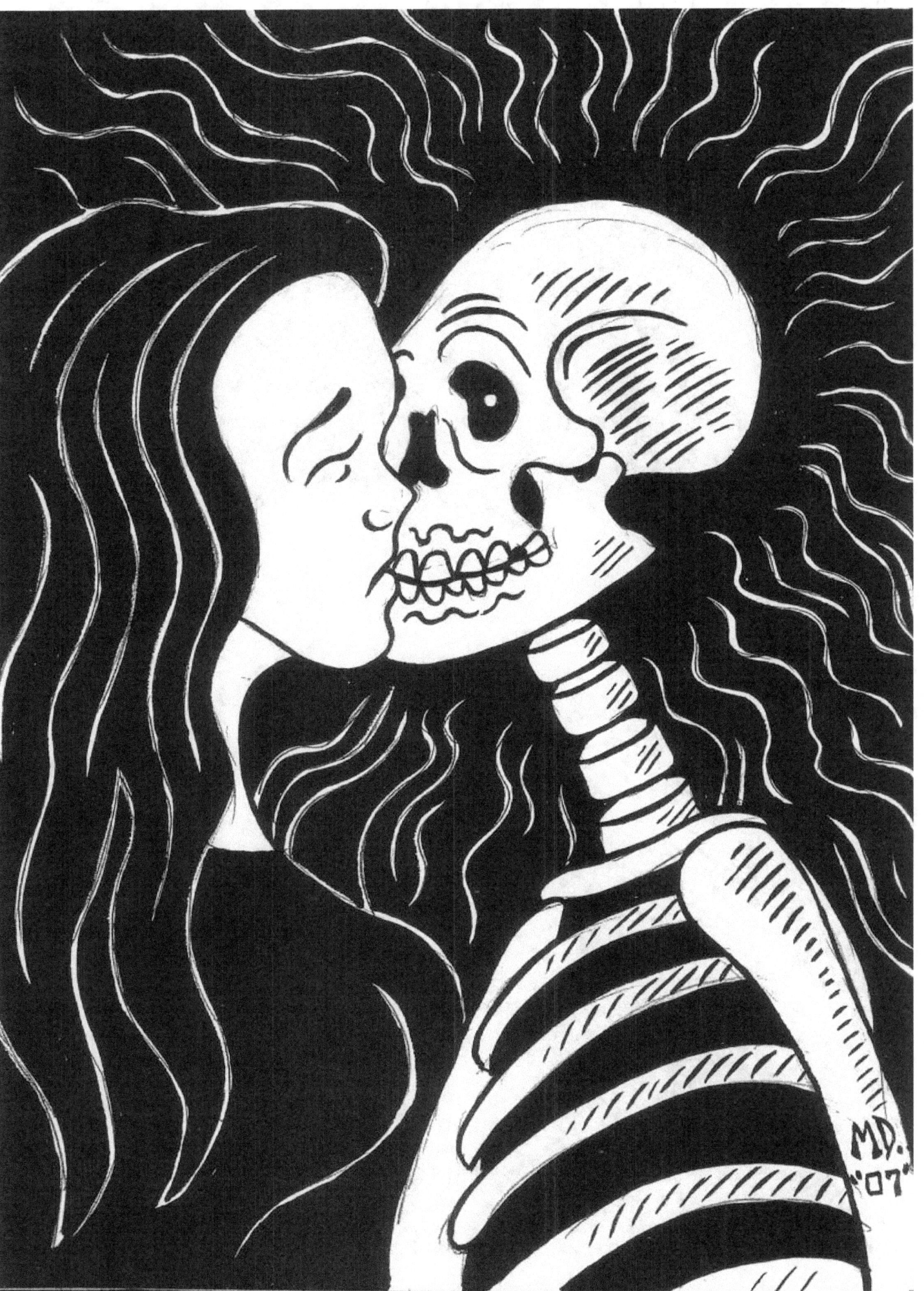

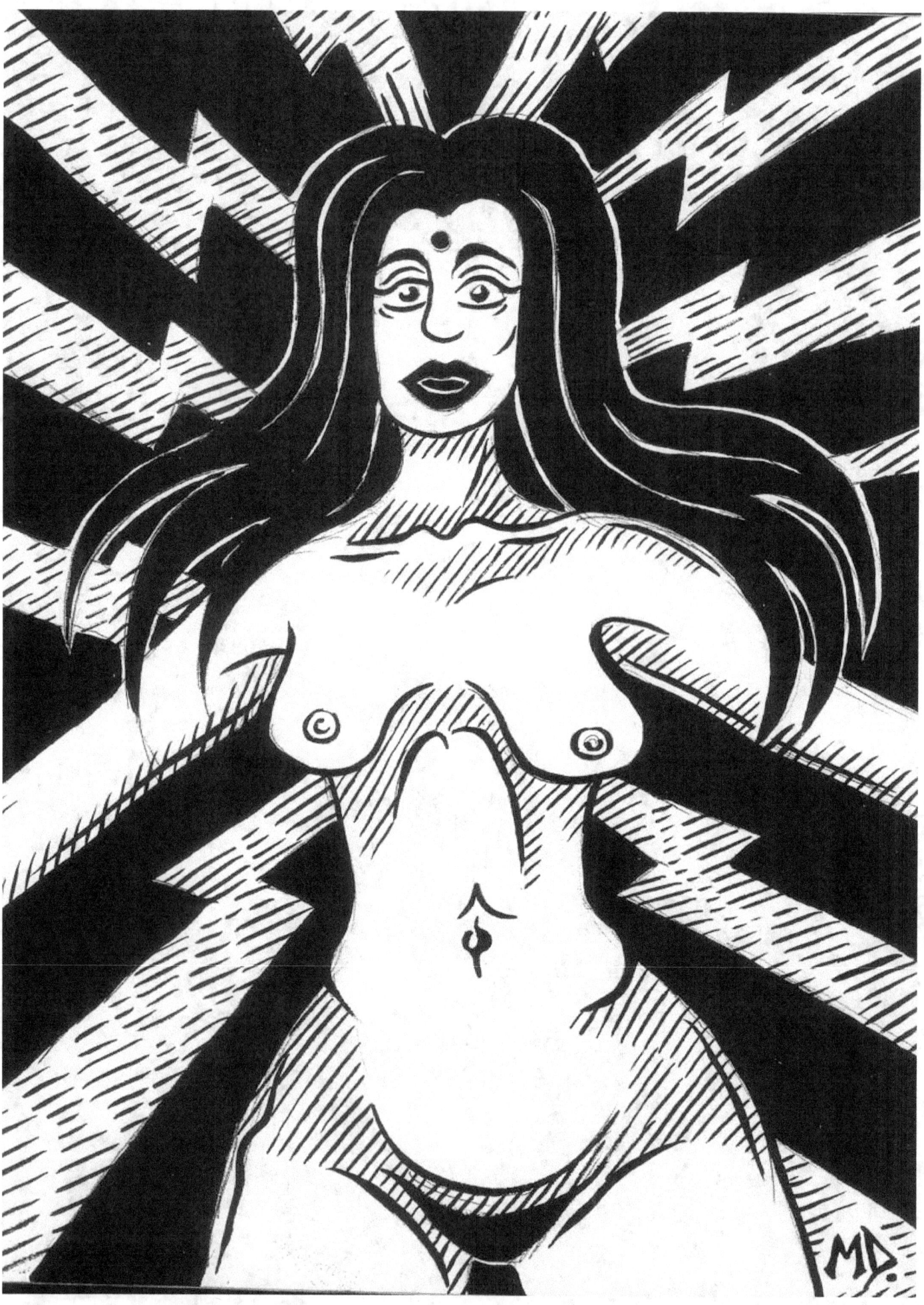

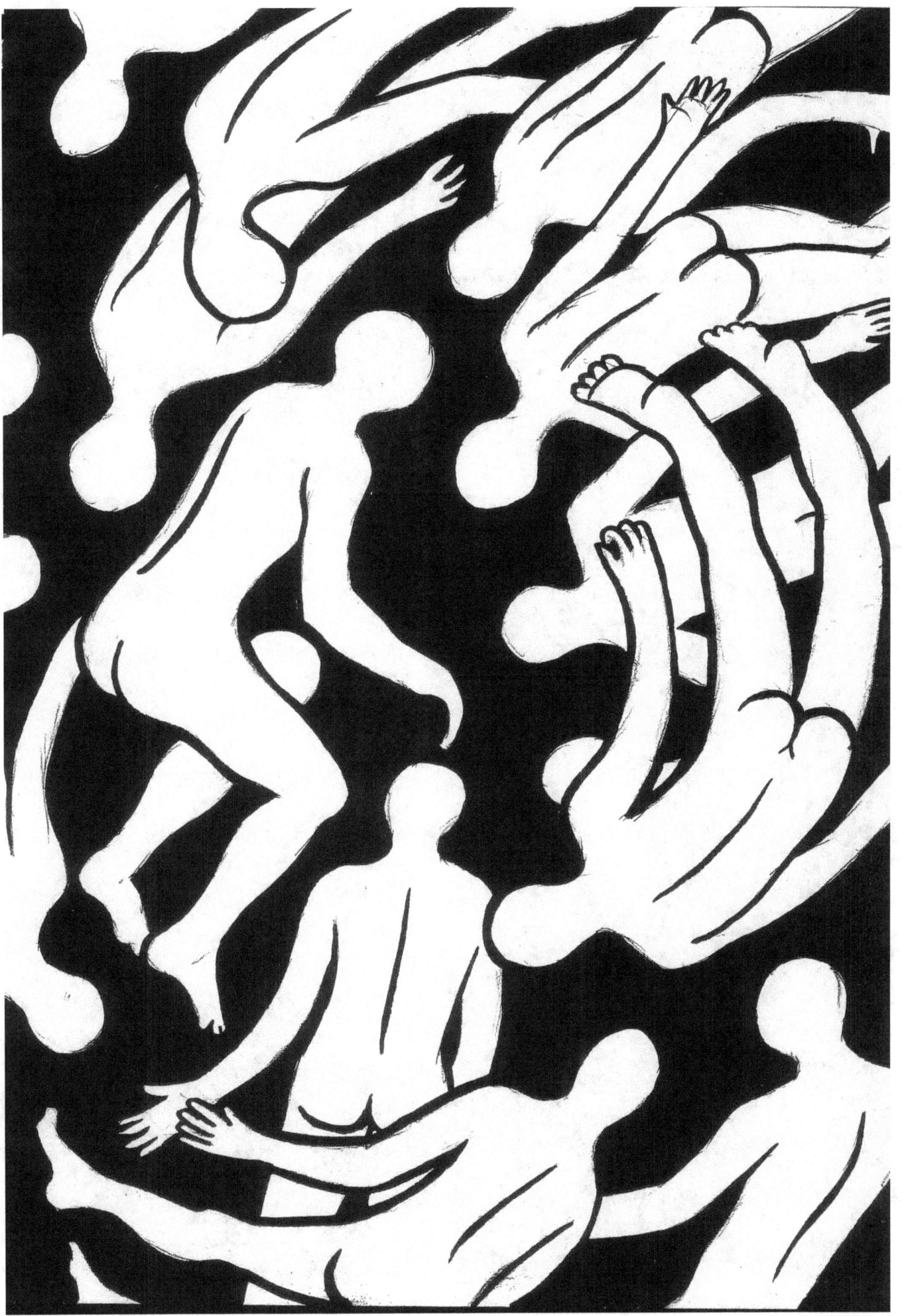

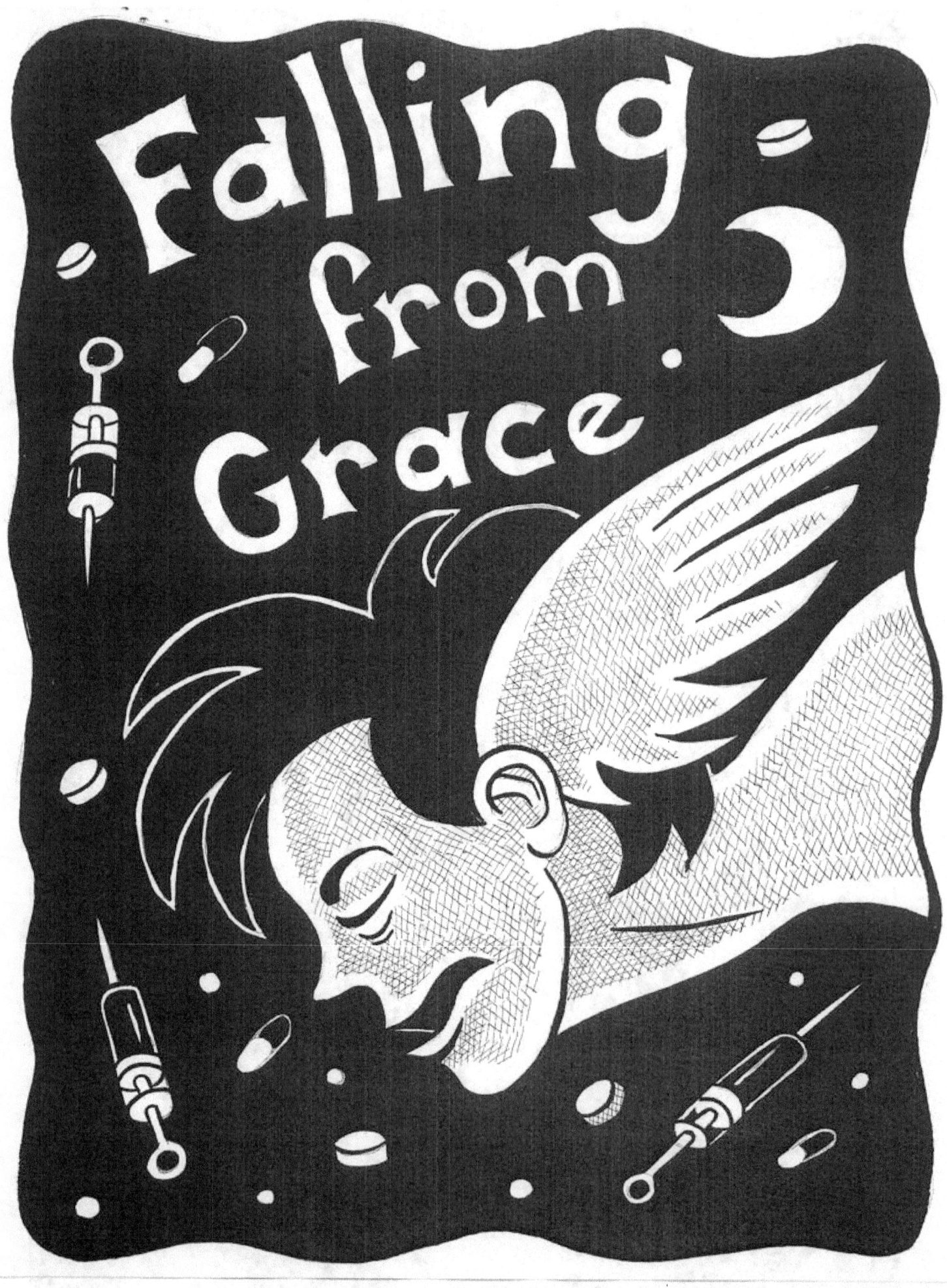

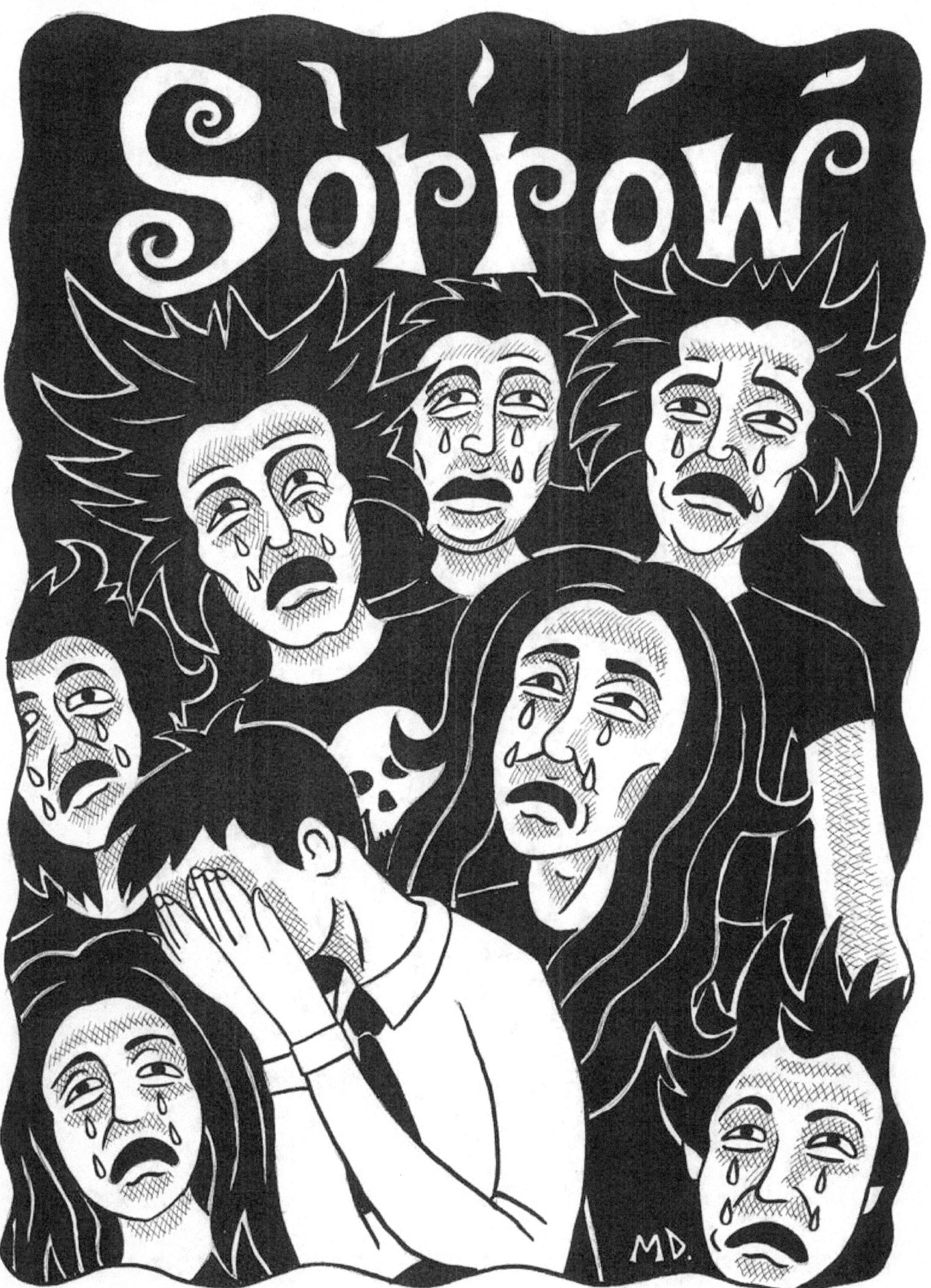

The Gate
CEMETARY
RIP
RIP
RIP
RIP
MD.

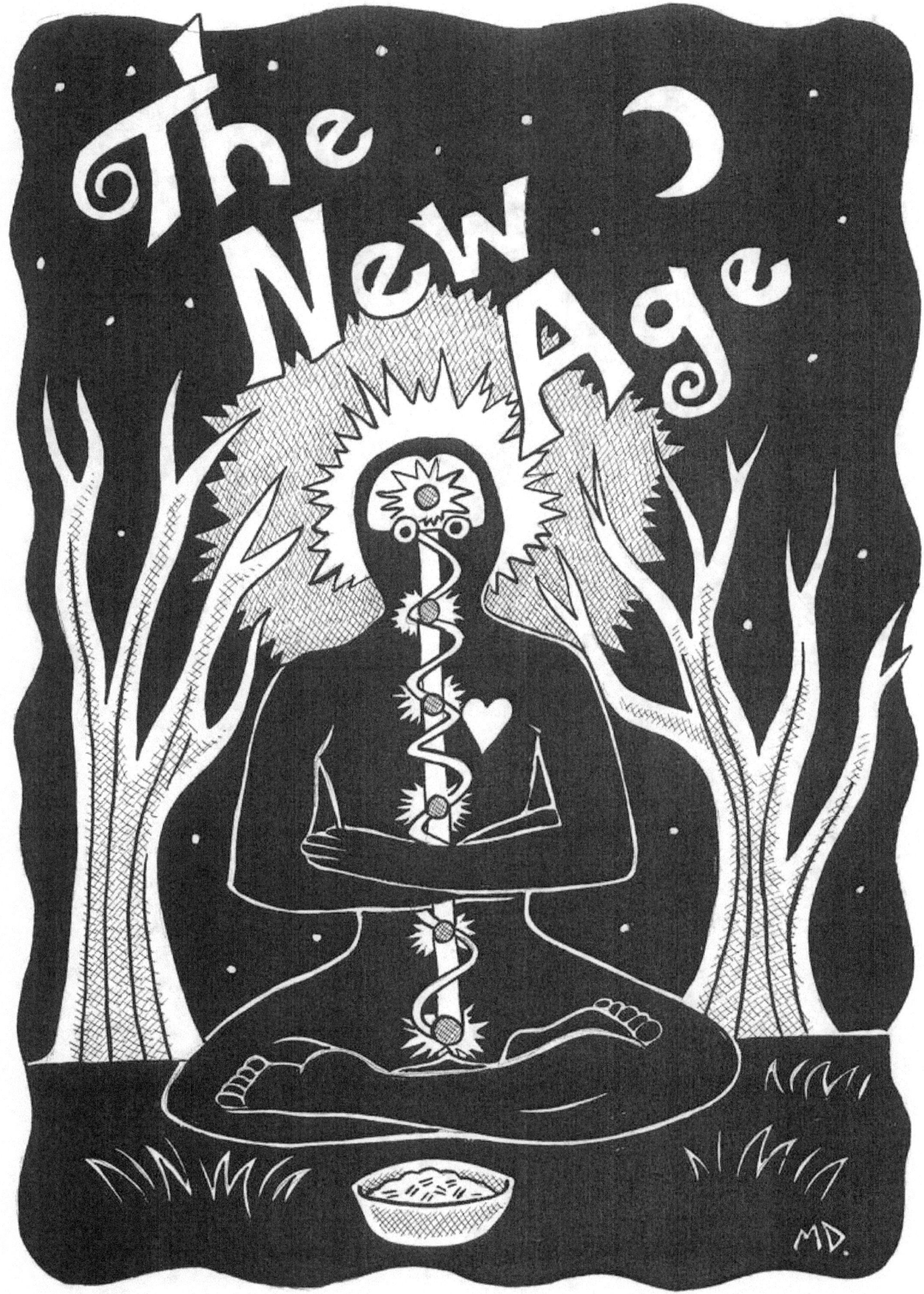

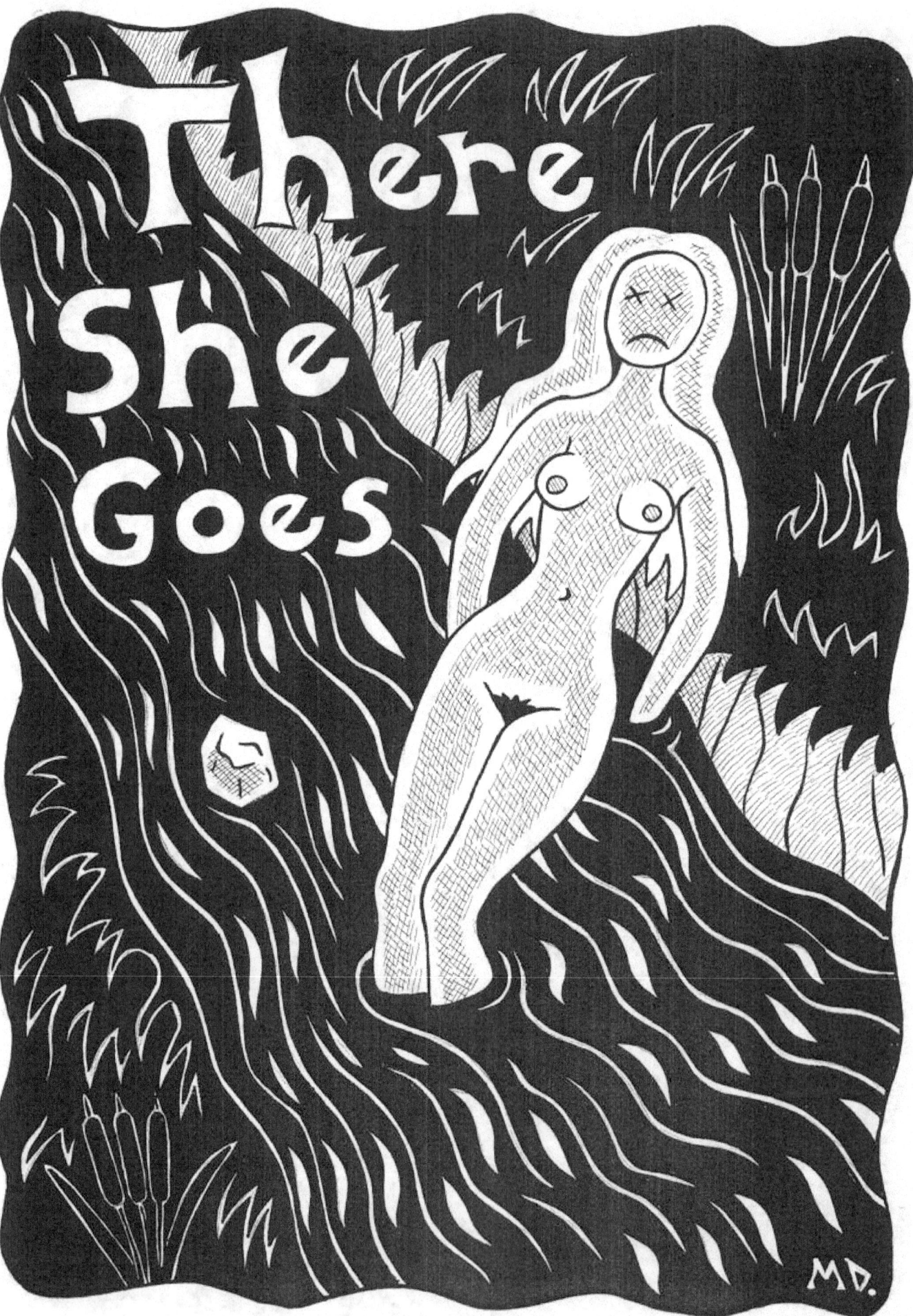

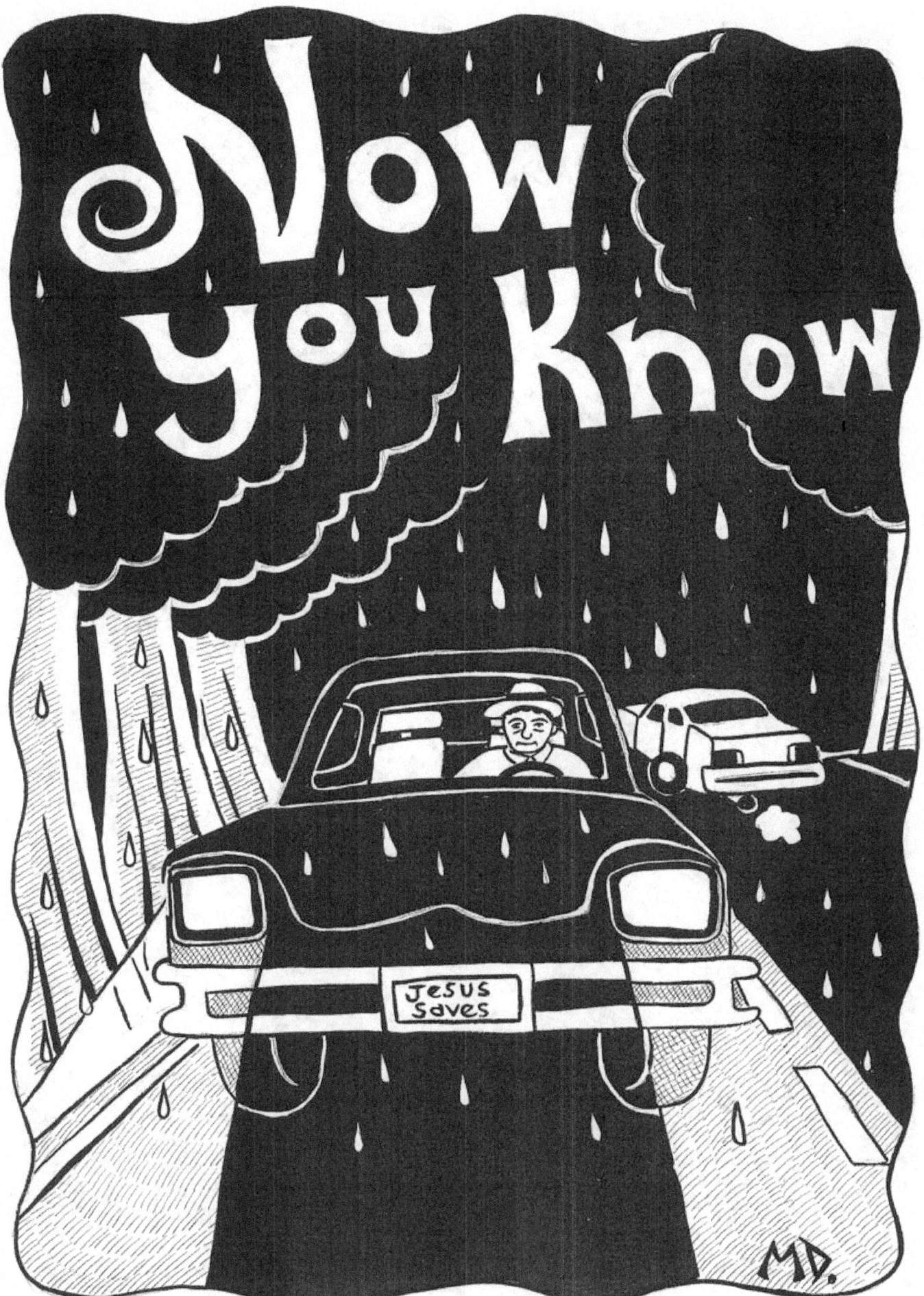

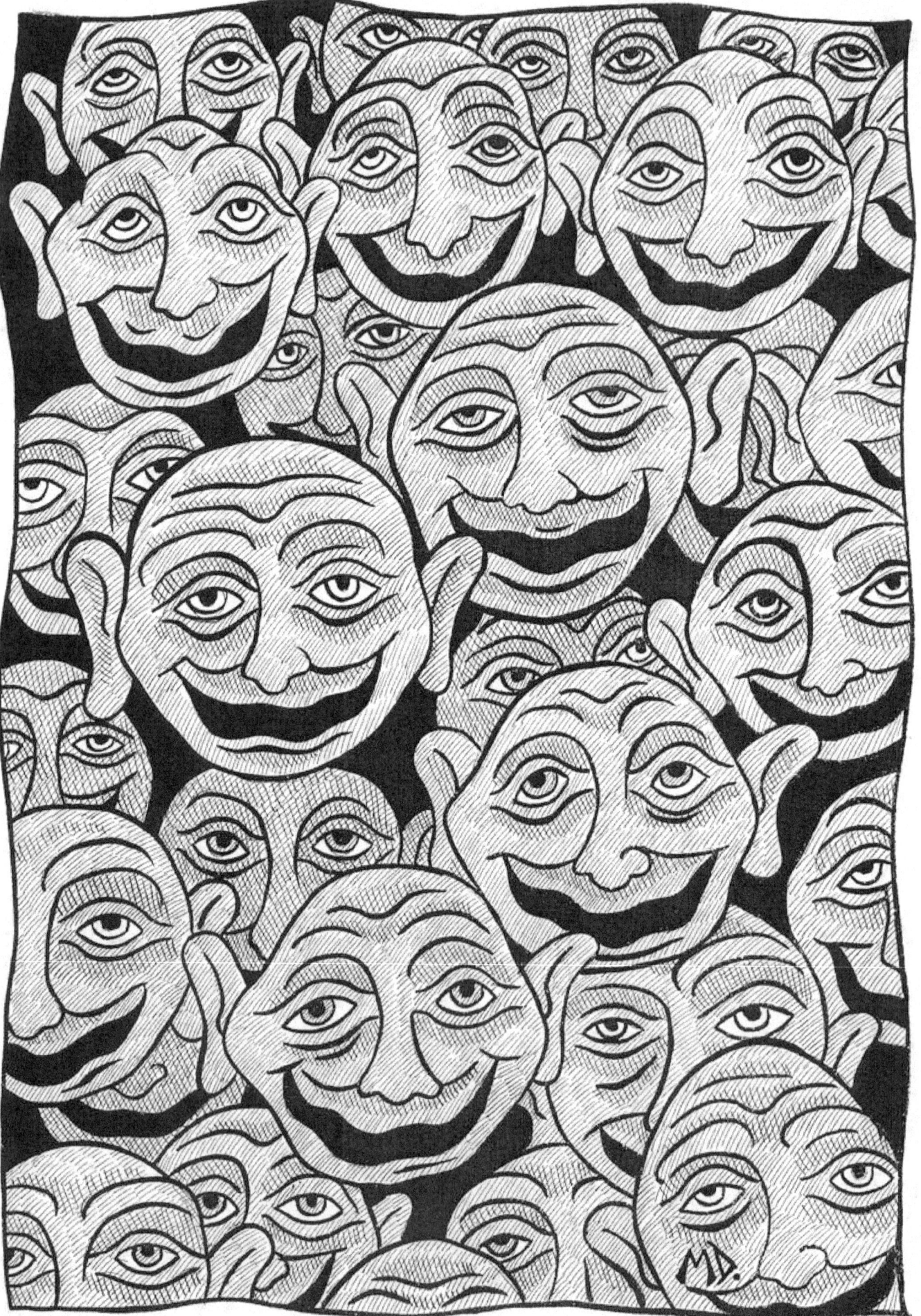

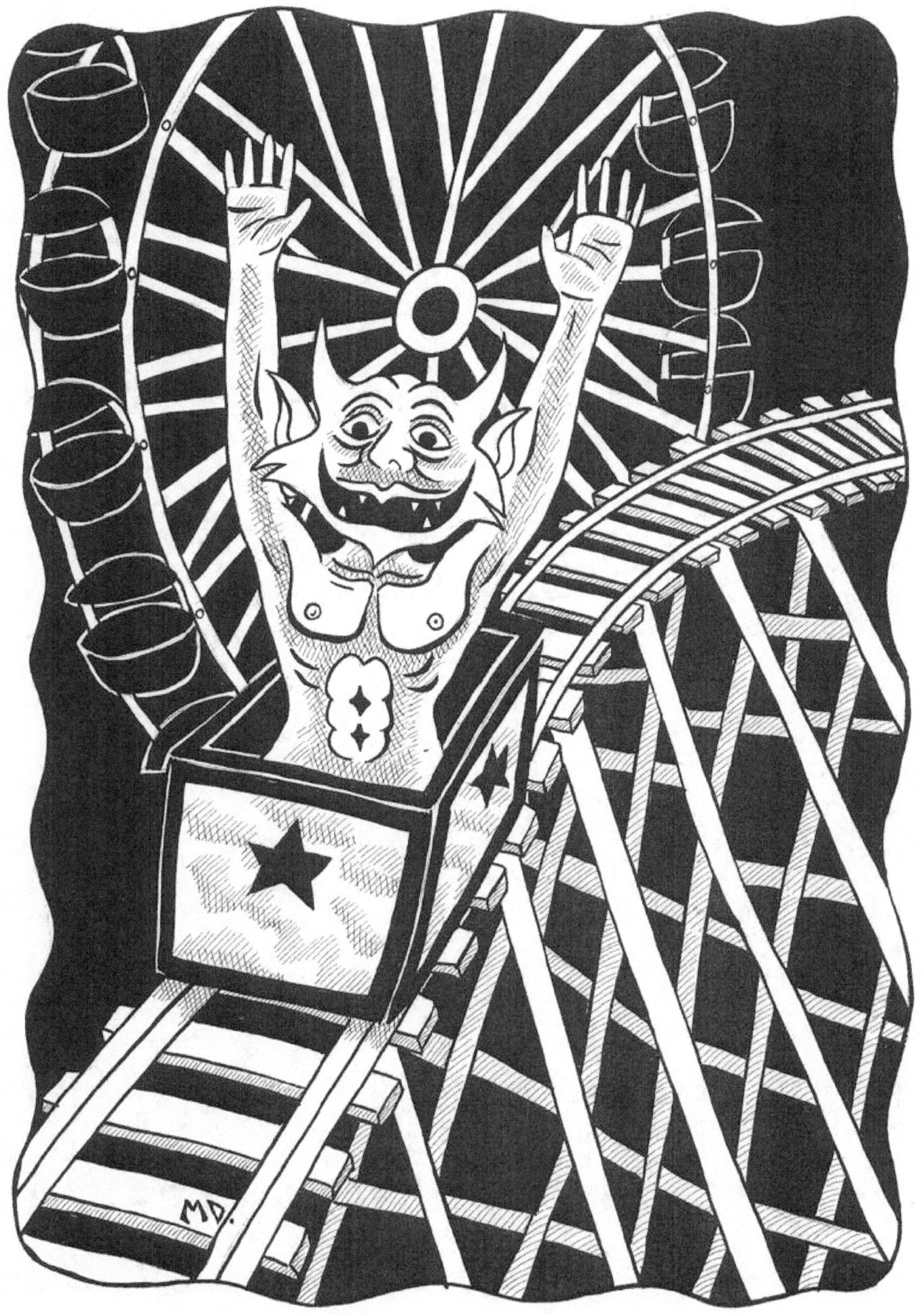

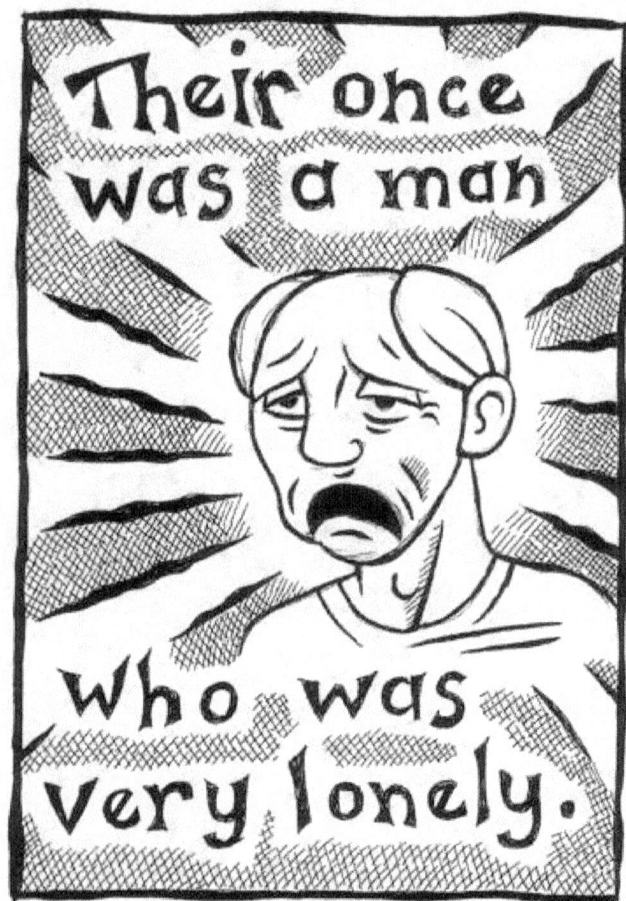

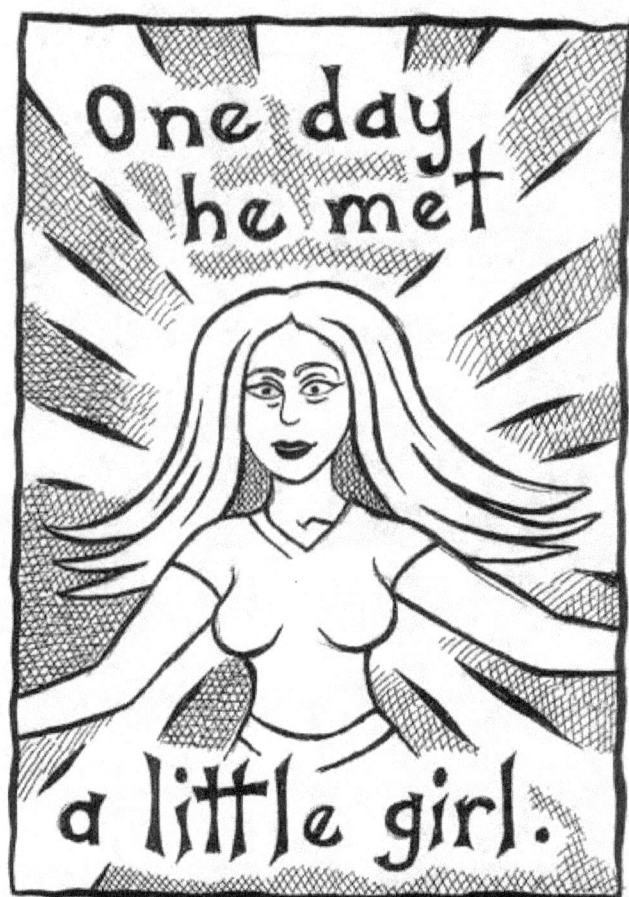

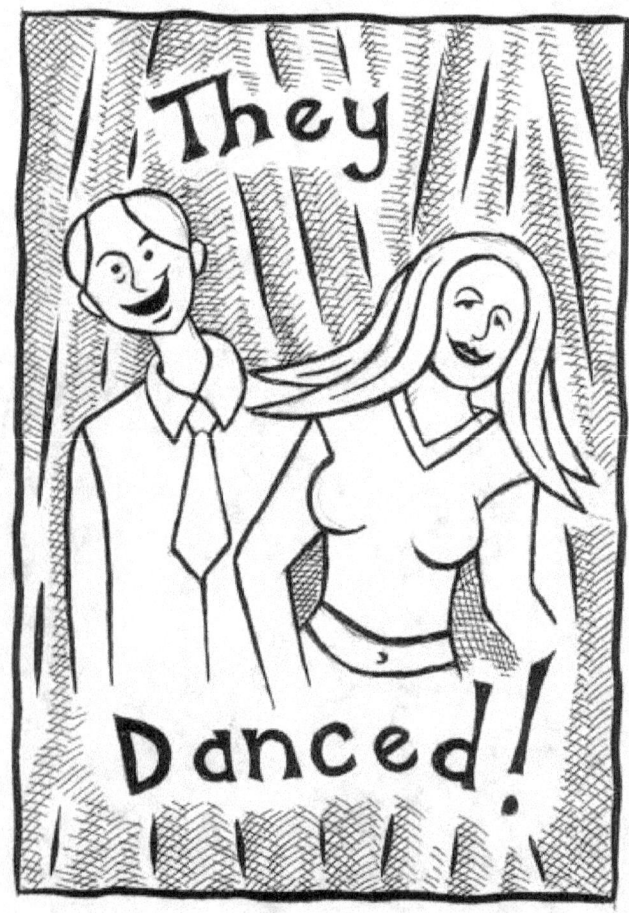

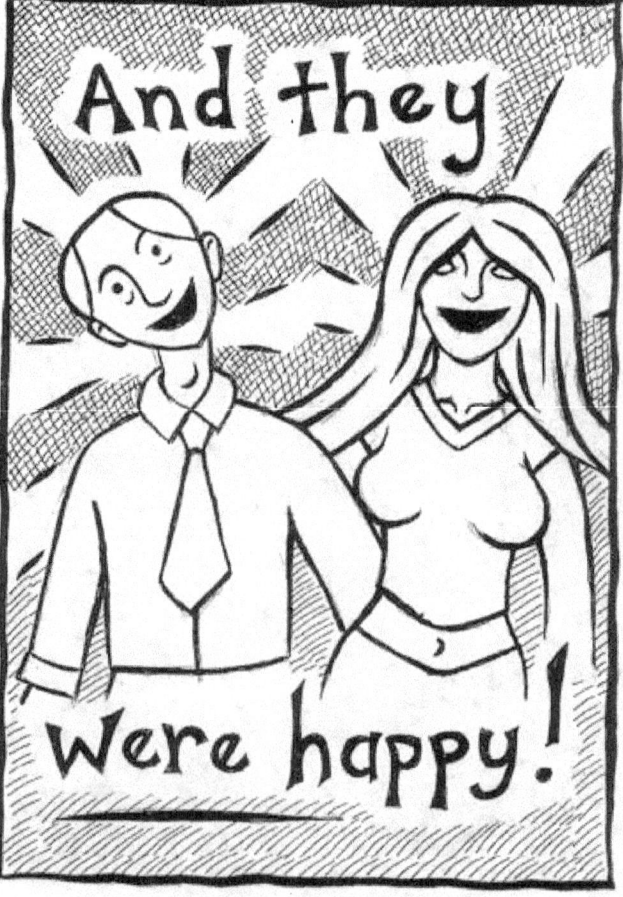

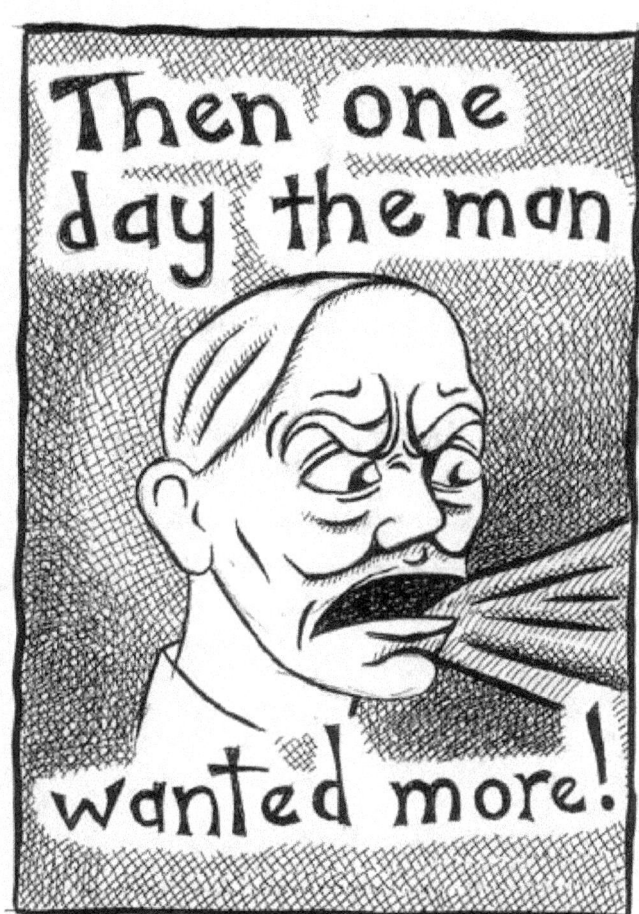

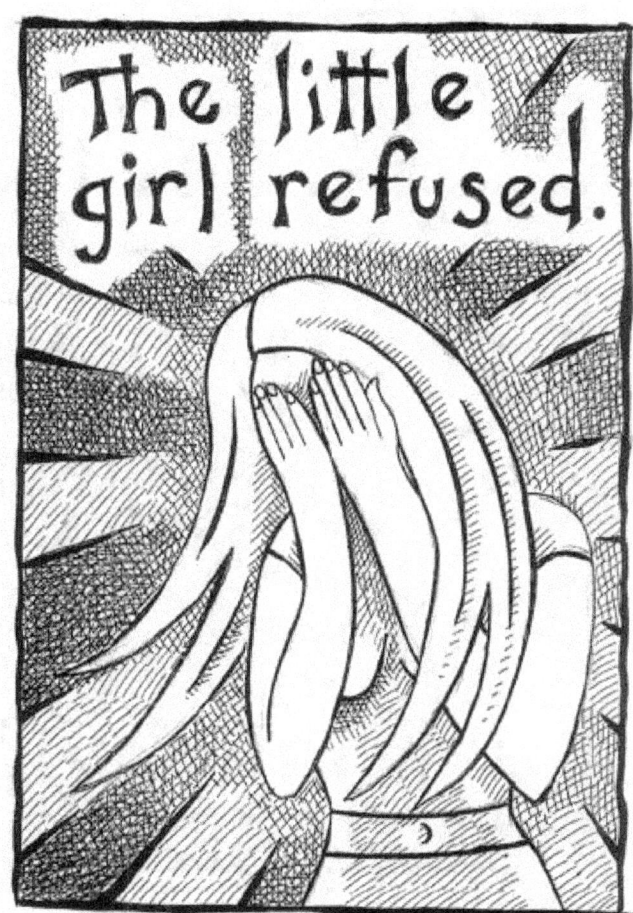

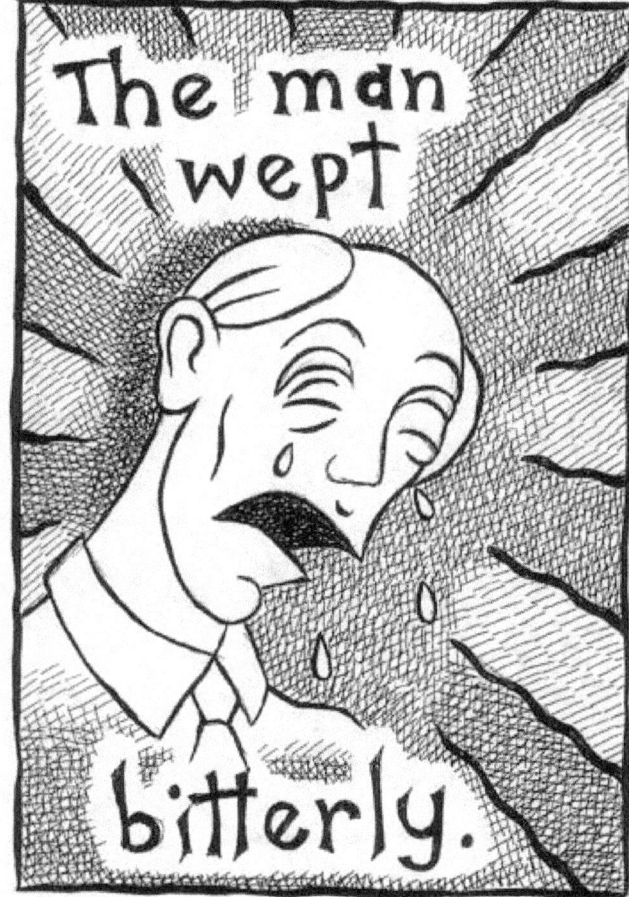

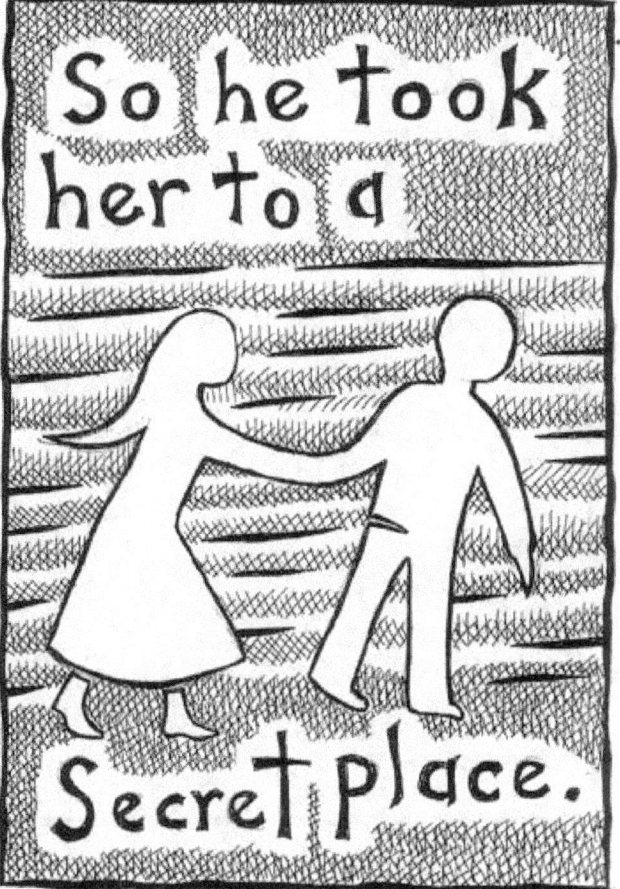

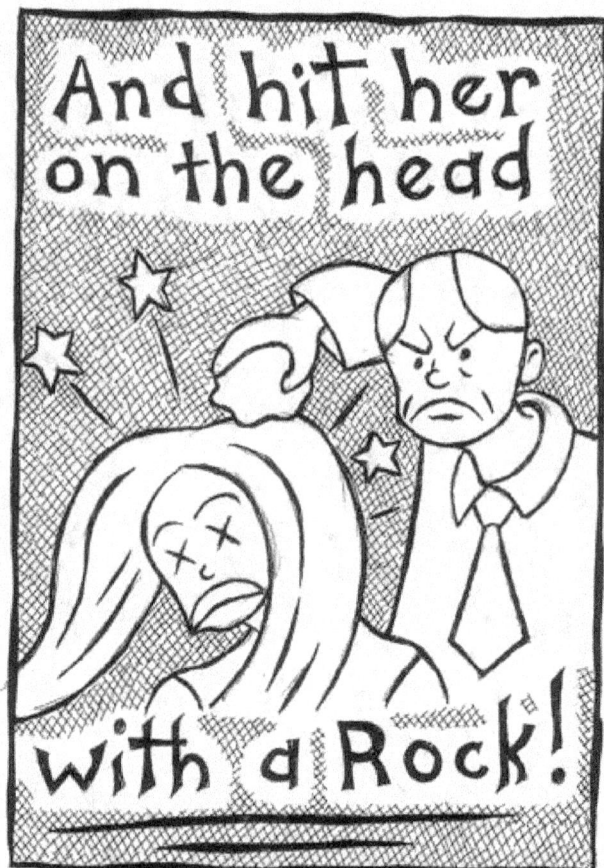

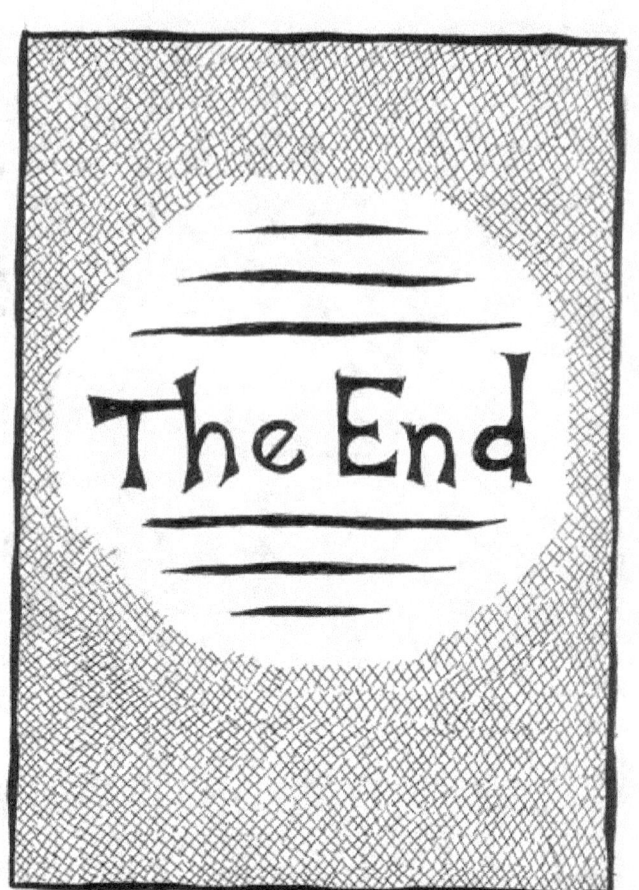

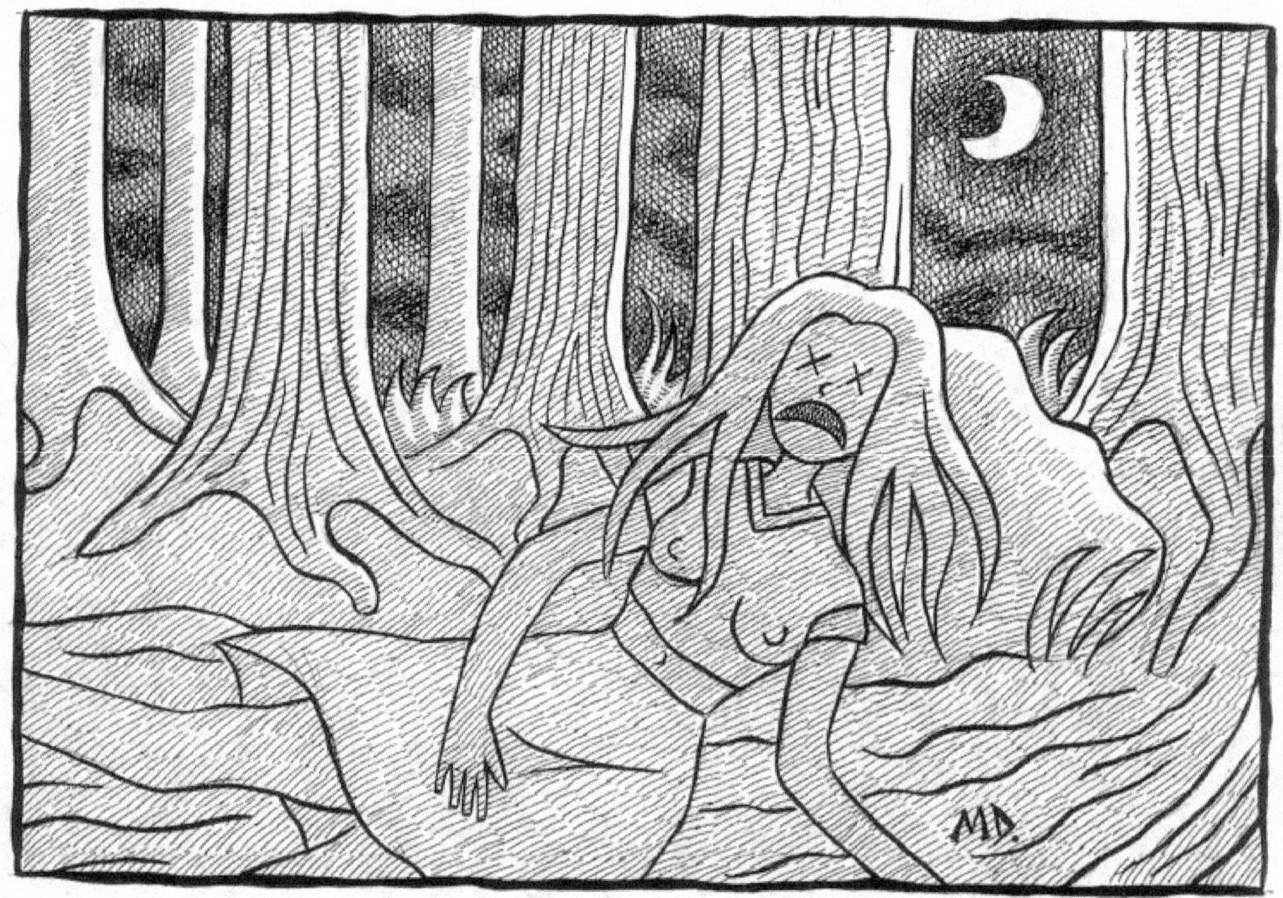

The End...

www.ingramcontent.com/pod-product-compliance
Lightning Source LLC
Chambersburg PA
CBHW080831310526
45788CB00019B/3097